the

KETO
GUIDEBOOK

A Proven Plan to Ditch Fake Foods,
Embrace a High-Fat Diet, & Become
a Healthy & Vibrant New You

by

Martina Johansson

VICTORY BELT PUBLISHING

Las Vegas

First Published in 2017 by Victory Belt Publishing Inc.

ISBN-13: 978-1-628601-28-2

The author is not a licensed practitioner, physician, or medical professional and offers no medical diagnoses, treatments, suggestions, or counseling. The information presented herein has not been evaluated by the U.S. Food and Drug Administration, and it is not intended to diagnose, treat, cure, or prevent any disease. Full medical clearance from a licensed physician should be obtained before beginning or modifying any diet, exercise, or lifestyle program, and physicians should be informed of all nutritional changes.

The author/owner claims no responsibility to any person or entity for any liability, loss, or damage caused or alleged to be caused directly or indirectly as a result of the use, application, or interpretation of the information presented herein.

Cover Design by Justin-Aaron Velasco

Interior Design by Yordan Terziev and Boryana Yordanova

Printed in Canada

TC 0318

Table of Contents

Introduction

Because you have picked up this book, you are probably interested in looking and feeling your best, as well as getting rid of any excess weight you might be carrying, kicking the sugar habit, and controlling inflammation. Today, most people suffer from food cravings, fatigue, stress, chronic illnesses, or pain, to name just a few common conditions. The fact that our society is highly *un*natural in nature is causing us to fall out of tune with our bodies and ourselves.

The first step toward a healthier you is to reclaim your hormonal and emotional signaling systems. A ketogenic diet excels at this task. But why?

The answer is straightforward. A ketogenic diet excels at reclaiming your hormonal and emotional signaling systems because it is a 100 percent natural eating plan that lets your body heal from the inside out by restoring functions at a cellular level. As a valuable bonus, excess weight is effortlessly lost. A body that's in balance does not want to be overweight because being overweight is a highly unnatural state, never seen in wild animals or indigenous people.

My personal keto journey began about seven years ago, when I was a university student majoring in biochemistry and genetic engineering. Even though I was fascinated by what I was learning, I could hardly keep my eyes open during lectures. I was always tired and unfocused; I slept too much and suffered from recurring colds and throat infections. My allergies were so severe during the spring and summer that I couldn't leave my home. Even though I maintained a normal weight, I wasn't fit at all. Because of my unwillingness to participate, I had difficulty passing physical education courses at school. I couldn't run or jump, and I was terrified of water, ball sports, and gymnastics. I was too weak for the gym and too uncoordinated for aerobics. Every gym class was a nightmare, which is why I graduated as a straight-A student with a D average in physical education.

During my university years, I began worrying about my poor physical health and weak constitution. I could barely run 100 yards without collapsing. The difficulty I had even summoning the energy to carry my books to school started to disturb me. I felt ill, and I was becoming convinced that something was seriously wrong with me. I went to the doctor for a checkup, but all the tests came back normal. This made me worry even more, because if there wasn't anything wrong with me, how could I do anything to improve how I was feeling? In my discouraged state, I decided to try all the vitamins and supplements I could find at the local pharmacy. I also resolved to buy only healthy foods at the supermarket, such as whole grains, oatmeal, brown rice, and low-fat dairy products. Although it seemed as though I was doing everything by the book, my body remained in an almost constant state of inflammation, and I kept feeling worse. My attention span was incredibly short, my thoughts were clouded, and I constantly felt unwell.

The turning point came a couple months later when I attended a class on environmental chemistry. The course itself didn't solve my health issues, but the professor made me look in a completely new direction for a solution. The professor was rabidly anti-sugar—so much so that he delivered a short admonition before each lecture about the detrimental effects of carbohydrates on our health. He even showed us newspaper articles in which he was interviewed or quoted for his radical statements about ice cream, processed foods, and margarine. Many of my classmates made fun of him by bringing fast foods and sweets to his lectures, but I believed that his message really was an important one. What he was saying resonated with me, even though I didn't dare to believe every word he said just yet.

My diet at that time consisted mainly of different types of carbohydrates, the barest minimum of protein, and no fat. I had become a vegetarian at age fifteen because it seemed healthier than the standard Western diet and because it eliminated a lot of junk food by default. However, when I moved out of my parents' home and into my student apartment, it was easier to throw something ready-made into the microwave or simply skip meals altogether and replace them with coffee and candy bars. Although my constant fatigue and brain fog forced me to try to survive entirely on caffeine and sugar for long periods, it was a poor nutritional bandage. This habit greatly affected my sleep and stomach health and contributed to my inflamed body.

At some level, I understood the connection between diet and health, but I wasn't knowledgeable enough to take adequate action. Vitamins and whole grains were a small step toward increased awareness, but unfortunately, they were a step in the wrong direction. When I had the opportunity to talk to my professor one-on-one, he was happy to lecture me on the connection between sugar and inflammation, poor immune system response, allergies, and all kinds of other issues that I could relate to my own life. My appetite for the subject grew. In addition to private lectures, I did an immense amount of online research, read academic articles, and participated in forum discussions. Everything I thought I knew about nutrition prior to talking with my professor turned out to be wrong, and it became clear that I needed to reconsider my entire lifestyle. The fact that I spent between twelve and sixteen hours a day in front of a computer screen, had a sky-high caffeine intake, and ate a carb-and-grain-based diet pointed to an urgent need for change. That much I knew.

The final straw was when I came across Dr. Nancy Appleton's book, *Suicide by Sugar.* In an intense state of fear and determination, I threw my entire food supply into the trash: my ready-made meals, candy bars, fat-free dairy products, cereals, oatmeal, and crackers. The new problem I faced was that I didn't know what to eat instead, especially as a vegetarian. However, I decided to throw myself into it and learn whatever I could along the way.

I began to scrutinize food labels, and it occurred to me for the first time how little real food most so-called food products contain. Many of my favorite products until then were little more than lists of chemicals. Even soy products and other seemingly "healthy" substitutes turned out to be over-processed and thoroughly unnatural. I added different types of natural foods to my diet, and I tried whole-fat dairy for the first time. My body reacted violently to the sudden drop in refined sugar and starch, and I suffered a variety of withdrawal symptoms, including headaches, mood swings, and a marked worsening of my fatigue. I understood that my body was detoxing, though, so I kept at it. After a couple weeks, I felt better than I'd ever felt before. My energy was increasing; I went from needing ten or twelve hours of sleep each night to managing perfectly well on about seven hours. My brain fog lessened, and I found that I could focus on my studies with much less effort. For the first time, I felt that I was *living* instead of just existing—and it made me curious about adding meat to my diet to see if it would improve my newfound well-being even more. I began with fish and some poultry, then dared to add pork and beef.

The new intake of protein with perfect biocompatibility made my nails and hair grow stronger and faster, and my previously pale skin developed a healthy glow. My energy levels peaked so high that I experienced an irresistible urge to exercise. Suddenly, I had a problem sitting still. I felt suffocated by the thought of spending twelve hours a day in front of a computer. This deer needed to run!

I started to run just 400 yards a day, at a pace slower than most people walk. I gradually increased the distance until I ran my first half-mile. One mile soon turned into several. A year later, I ran my first 10K race, and two years after that, my first marathon. I couldn't believe how good it felt to be filled with energy and vitality, just as any twenty-five-year-old should expect to feel all the time.

A little more than seven years has passed, and my health and fitness continue to improve each year. I began serious gym training a few years ago, and since 2012 I have been competing internationally in both weight lifting and fitness. It's amazing how the right nutrition can be such a game-changer. Equally amazing is how processed and unnatural foods can destroy so much of a human being's potential.

I wrote this book because I realized that most people don't know what it feels like to live in a state of peak fitness and health. Although not everything boils down to nutrition, it's a very basic concept that can immeasurably improve all sorts of things. I'm passionate about helping people tap into their unknown strengths, and I strongly believe that following a ketogenic diet is a safe and efficient way to do so. Regardless of your personal goals, age, and health status, a ketogenic approach can help you improve in many areas and reconnect with your inner signaling system.

If you don't feel your best, there's a reason for it, and I dedicate this book to you. You deserve to have great health and limitless energy, and I sincerely hope that you will give the advice in this book a fair try. Bear in mind that most processed foods manipulate gut and brain function to an extent that we no longer know whether we are hungry or satisfied. They make us feel stressed out, overly emotional, and in a permanent state of fight-or-flight. They put a lot of stress on our endocrine systems and gradually make us sick, fat, and foggy. The truth is that most people can't process these industrialized foods, but the decline in well-being occurs so gradually that most of us don't even think to link our problems to the food we are consuming.

Because processed foods are frequently highly allergenic and inflammatory, they can manipulate the body into releasing powerful chemicals. These chemicals have addictive qualities and can cause us to binge-eat or develop addictions to certain foods. If you don't recognize an ingredient, there's a good chance that your body won't, either; consuming it will do you no favors.

Pharmaceutical companies have been trying to develop a pill for every modern-day disease, but most of these ailments stem from the same source: inflammation. As research progresses, more and more diseases, syndromes, and conditions turn out to be the result of prolonged inflammation. Inflammation ceases to exist when we start feeding our bodies the foods they are designed to eat. Easier said than done, you might think—especially when we can no longer distinguish real food from fake. Fruit is a great example of a food that looks, smells, and tastes natural, but in reality is highly modified and has an unnaturally high fructose (sugar) content.

"Healthy" slogans and symbols on packaging are another way we are conned into buying processed foods that undermine our health. In this book, I hope to guide you toward a better understanding of what different types of foods really do to your body. I will show you what to avoid and what to include for maximum health benefits.

I will explain in more detail how the ketogenic diet works and how to smoothly integrate it into your life. I will discuss hormone optimization, strategic meal planning, and physical exercise that is suitable for people at all fitness levels. I explore the principles of human metabolism and show you how you can use them to your advantage without having to count calories ever again. In the second half of the book, I share my favorite recipes to get you started and give you motivating results fast. I believe in learning by doing, so don't be afraid to experiment and try things out for yourself. It will be easy as soon as you grasp the central concepts. When eating ketogenic, it's more important to listen to your body than to follow a set of rules—so remember to look inside and do what makes you feel good.

The ketogenic diet is an intuitive and relaxed way of getting into shape that is much more in tune with your body's actual needs than any other diet or trendy eating plan. It's completely stress-free, and it doesn't require you to spend hours on the treadmill or endure endless hunger. Restricting calories and doing strenuous cardio are not lasting solutions, nor are they especially effective. Fitness and health should never feel like punishment. I believe in integrating activities and foods that are in tune with your true nature instead of doing things that don't make you feel any better—or actually make you feel bad. We have enough obligations already; exercising shouldn't be one of them.

Remember that your cells communicate with you every minute of the day, and one key to health is to listen to those messages. When your health deteriorates, it's a sign that you have already ignored several warning signals, or that you cured the symptoms rather than addressing what was causing them. Those warning signs could include pain, weight gain, recurring colds or infections, stomach issues, mood swings, depression, anxiety, or brain fog, to name just a few. Whatever the signals, they all say the same thing: something you are doing consistently is not working for you, and it's your job to find out what it is. It would be convenient if our bodies could just explain the problem to us, but unfortunately we need to apply a little guesswork and explore different approaches until we get to the right answer. We can't count on doctors to solve everything for us. We are better off learning a little bit about our biochemistry so that we can feel good without painkillers.

Don't be deceived when it comes to health. We all have the ability to look our best and lead healthy, happy lives, despite genes or external circumstances. Addictive and inflammatory foods really mess up our internal signaling system and increase our risk of making bad choices. We compensate for poor sleep with caffeine, and we continue to eat way past the sensation of fullness. We eat for comfort and to ease stress, or perhaps we "binge" on certain foods. This leads to a continuous feeling of vague discontentment that could manifest itself in the body as disease if left unheeded.

Society has led us to believe that if we run on the treadmill long enough, we can eat whatever we want and either lose weight or remain healthy—as though unhealthy food in excess doesn't count as long as we compensate with strenuous workouts. Nothing could be further from the truth. The calorie is not a static unit, and the body is orchestrated by a finely tuned hormonal system that shouldn't be corrupted. If you do corrupt it, you will likely gain weight or compromise your health in some other way.

Even though more people go to the gym than ever before, obesity is skyrocketing. This is because it is impossible to counteract poor lifestyle choices and food addictions with physical exercise. Exercise is a wonderful therapy because humans are designed for movement. However, it won't make you thin. If you merely want to lose weight, you would do better to start by healing your body from within with an anti-inflammatory diet. In general, nutritional choices account for more than 70 percent of weight-loss successes, as well as gains in fitness and strength. Resistance training is a great tool for shaping and toning muscles, while chronic cardio is more of a negative stressor.

The key is to find joy in movement, as well as to lower your expectations of what working out should look like. You don't need fancy fitness clothes, smart watches, pedometers, or jogging shoes equipped with the latest technology. You just need to get up, get moving, and break the harmful habit of a sedentary lifestyle. If you sit at a desk for several hours a day, you will come home exhausted and might end up in front of the TV before you go to bed. That's a very unnatural way to live, and it is a risk factor for many modern lifestyle diseases.

Physical exercise isn't always fun, but it's necessary for optimal health. We are designed to run, walk, swim, throw, jump, lift, and climb for several hours a day, which is why sitting in a chair for extended periods is so unnatural that it weakens your body and causes your general health to deteriorate. Natural exercise needs to be accompanied by natural foods—the types of foods that humans have been eating for eons. After reading this book, you will begin to regard colorful packaging and "healthy" slogans as warning signs, because truly healthy food cannot be branded and doesn't need labels.

In addition to its wonderful anti-inflammatory properties, a ketogenic diet is also the most efficient way to burn body fat. Chapters 2, 3, and 7 explain how this process works. Ketogenic eating is rapidly gaining in popularity as more and more people are using it to successfully battle both obesity and "chronic" conditions such as type 2 diabetes, epilepsy, PCOS (polycystic ovary syndrome), IBS (irritable bowel syndrome), hypertension, and heart disease. This book will help you duplicate these successes by arming you with the knowledge you need in order to avoid common pitfalls. If you follow the steps and dedicate yourself wholeheartedly to the process, I promise that you will never again have to resort to calorie-counting and self-deprivation. Those other diets are part of the problem that caused your weight and health issues in the first place!

AFTER READING THIS BOOK YOU WILL:

- Understand why you haven't reached your goal weight/dream body yet

- Get practical tools to become your healthiest and best-looking self

- Understand the fundamentals of hormonal weight loss and acquire fascinating knowledge about the insulin and glycemic indexes and how to use them to your advantage

- Familiarize yourself with what a ketogenic diet really is and the health benefits you can expect to gain from it

- Understand that neither weight loss nor exercise needs to be complicated or stressful, but are things that anyone can do regardless of age or condition

- Learn how to cook anti-inflammatory meals to heal your body and get rid of food cravings

Are you ready to become a healthy and vibrant new you?
Let's get the transformation started!

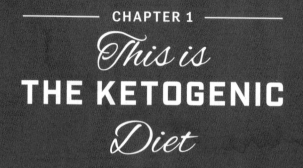

> *Nobody had ever told me junk food was*
> *bad for me. Four years of medical school,*
> *and four years of internship and residency,*
> *and I never thought anything was wrong*
> *with eating sweet rolls and doughnuts, and*
> *potatoes, and bread, and sweets.*

—ROBERT ATKINS

The truth is that most medical doctors don't learn much about nutrition or human metabolism in medical school. That means most MDs don't relate their patients' health conditions to their eating habits. Many common conditions can easily be treated with lifestyle changes, and you will soon understand how and why. In this chapter, I will discuss the ketogenic diet in more detail so that you understand what it is, how it works, and why it is superior to other ways of eating. This is a pretty comprehensive subject, so I will continue to delve into various aspects of this diet over the next few chapters. Here, I'll start with the basics.

The Atkins diet has been popular for several decades. However, it has encountered a lot of criticism, including accusations of commercialism. The Atkins diet was charged with being unethical and even dangerous in the long term. Also in this chapter, I will take a closer look at the Atkins diet and the ways in which a ketogenic diet differs.

DIFFERENT TYPES OF "LOW-CARB"

Limiting carbohydrate intake is a fast and easy way to feel better and lose weight. However, many people need more information to make it work. It helps to have some knowledge of basic biochemistry, macronutrients, and nutritional values as well as a sound understanding of human metabolism.

Dr. Robert Atkins, the creator of the Atkins diet, was very overweight and had a large appetite. When he heard that he could lose weight without restricting calories, he knew that this was the only choice for him. When he quit junk food and limited his carb intake, he lost the excess weight in a matter of months and became aware of the hormonal effects that his dietary changes had on his body. He understood that he could effectively wipe diabetes from the surface of the earth if he could get everyone to eat like this!

In truth, a strict low-carb diet was the common treatment for diabetes before scientists could synthesize insulin. Insulin, however, was a more profitable way to treat the disease without requiring patients to make dietary changes. Dr. Atkins began recommending the diet to his patients, and they saw good results by following in his footsteps. He started to write books and cookbooks, and the Atkins diet grew into an empire.

When the diet was developed into a commercial brand and Atkins turned away from natural foods, a lot of its integrity was lost. If you go to a supermarket nowadays, you can find candy bars, smoothies, cookies, and chocolate bars with the Atkins name on them, as well as soups and other calorie-restricted meal replacements. These products are highly processed, unnatural, and full of additives with long names that are incompatible with optimal health.

The Atkins diet focuses mainly on carb restriction, which is just a small piece of the puzzle. Because of this focus, it's totally understandable that many people try the diet for a short time and then give it up.

WHAT IS A KETOGENIC DIET?

A ketogenic diet is geared primarily toward natural and unprocessed foods that are free of additives. It cannot be commercialized; if it is, then it's not a ketogenic diet. Carb restriction is an inevitable part of the diet because natural foods are naturally low in carbohydrates. If a food is nutritious and natural but happens to have a higher carbohydrate content, it should not be excluded, because that's not the primary goal. The basic principles are violated when unnatural and man-made foods are chosen over natural products on the often-shaky premise of lower carb content. If you are eager to know more about which foods are ketogenic, you can find a list on pages 290 and 291.

Atkins has become synonymous with *low-carb* (or what people generally think of as low-carb). It's a diet with little sugar and lots of protein. Because many people are still terrified about the idea of adding fat to their diet, most low-carb enthusiasts focus on lean protein, vegetables, nuts, berries, and fruits. The reasoning seems to be that if low-carb is good, then low-carb, low-fat must be even better. This is erroneous thinking. Animal fats and natural vegetable fats, such as coconut oil, are among the most natural and healthiest things a person can eat.

Paleolithic and raw-food diets emerged as a reaction to low-carb diets that were subsequently taken over by food companies that wanted to make money with quick-fix products. The idea behind Paleo and raw-food diets is to go back to the most natural way of eating—the way people ate when humankind was more in touch with nature and lived as hunters and gatherers. These diets generally include a wide variety of vegetables, fruits, nuts, berries, animal proteins, and fats and exclude sugar, grains, and various dairy products. The key is to avoid anything unnatural so that the body gets 100 percent pure, nutritious food from high-quality sources at every meal. It's a great idea that truly works for a lot of people.

LOW-CARB VS. HIGH-FAT

About ten years ago, interest in low-carb diets started to emerge in Scandinavia because a Swedish medical doctor named Annika Dahlqvist rediscovered its effectiveness for weight loss and the treatment of diabetes. Dahlqvist tried a low-carb diet on herself first. She was pleased with the results, so she started recommending it to her patients, too. This approach was controversial at the time, and it led to a lot of media attention that contributed to increased curiosity in many people. Dahlqvist's low-carb diet grew into a grassroots movement that those with collected knowledge and insight decided to call the Low-Carb, High-Fat (LCHF) diet. They chose this name over simply "Low-Carb" to emphasize the importance of including natural and healthy fats. Despite the English name, it's a Swedish invention.

The stigma started to fade, and Annika Dahlqvist was no longer the only doctor encouraging patients to eat LCHF, which is very similar to the Atkins diet but brings an increased awareness of the health benefits of natural fats and whole-fat dairy. Today, more than a quarter of Swedes claim to eat a low-carb, high-fat diet. In the last decade, hundreds of books have been published about it. It is popularly described as a "health revolution" because it has revolutionized the health of millions of people, and more and more of us are understanding the benefits of adopting a more natural way of eating. However, almost any diet that utilizes fewer processed foods and less sugar and grains instantly improves most people's weight, mood, and well-being.

THE EMPHASIS ON FAT

As mentioned previously, most low-carb diets generally do not place much emphasis on fats, but rather focus on complex carbs and proteins. Most natural diets, such as the Paleo diet, are lower in carbohydrates. However, diets that substitute aspartame and other sweet chemical additives for sugar are low-carb, too, though these artificial sweeteners are poor health choices. Some of these diets embrace low-sugar foods that actually contain a liberal amount of carbohydrates, as different types of carbs are separated in a way that allows for a higher intake. One example of this is the idea of *net carbs*.

WHAT, THEN, ARE NET CARBS?

Manufacturers employ the concept of net carbs as a way of adding sugar to products without allowing the customer to see how much sugar those products actually contain. The quantities of sugar alcohols, fibers, and glycerin are subtracted from the total grams of carbohydrates in the product, and the different types of sugars are listed individually on the label. Net carbs are then said to be the carbs that have the biggest impact on blood sugar. However, this equation is not entirely accurate because many sugar alcohols and fibers are absorbed by the body. The modern Atkins diet focuses a lot on net carbs. Because these sugar alcohols and fibers occur only in industrialized foods, it is best to avoid them.

Complex carbs such as sweet potatoes, avocados, peas, beans, and root vegetables are preferred because they are more natural and therefore more easily processed by the body. Complex carbs can be included in a liberal low-carb diet that usually allows up to 150 grams of carbohydrates a day, which is suitable for fit people without any inflammatory diseases.

A ketogenic diet is much more restrictive when it comes to carb sources and quantities, and care is taken with the composition of each meal. Dairy products other than butter are usually omitted. When I started my keto journey six years ago, I dove into LCHF and ate a lot of whipped cream, crème fraîche, cheese, and full-fat yogurt. But as I learned more about my body, I began to understand why dairy foods in excess are not the way to optimal health. Dairy products, especially processed ones, can be quite inflammatory. Many scientific studies show that their effect on human growth hormone can increase the risk of cancer. Weight loss is much easier to attain when dairy is excluded, and psychological issues such as brain fog, cravings, and fatigue are wiped out almost immediately.

The main problem with dairy is that digestive enzymes in the small intestines break down milk proteins, such as casein, into casomorphins (peptides with highly addictive qualities). This phenomenon is known as molecular mimicry because the casomorphin is mimicking morphine molecules, binding to the opioid receptor sites in the brain. This is why many people—myself included—have a hard time giving up dairy or accepting its inflammatory and addictive qualities. Even though my pre-keto diet was high in refined sugars, nothing was more difficult than giving up yogurt, milky coffee, and whipped cream. I'm glad I did, though, because it revolutionized my mental clarity and fitness level.

The vegetables included in the ketogenic diet typically grow above ground—particularly cruciferous vegetables that are high in sulfur. Algae is a wonderful source of chlorophyll and other invigorating nutrients. I'm not going to discuss the metabolic processes of the keto diet just yet, but speaking of sulfur, low acidity is another important aspect of health. One of the reasons people were skeptical of the Atkins diet was the claim that excess protein and no carbs make the body acidic—like an acidified lake in which no life can prevail. This is a stubborn rumor without much truth to it. A lot of keto-approved vegetables, such as leafy greens, cabbage, and onions, are actually highly alkaline, which neutralize acids. Truly acidic things include carbonated water, soda, processed carbs, grains, and refined sugar.

FATS AND CALORIES

The most logical step for anyone who wants to lose weight is to decrease calorie intake. However, as I mentioned in the introduction to this book, decreasing calorie intake is an outdated and oversimplified way of looking at weight loss. A more modern approach is to consider the effects of different types of food on the gut flora, hormone system, brain, and blood sugar. This approach is a bit more complicated at first, but you will understand everything in due course.

One gram of fat contains 9 calories; 1 gram of protein contains 4 calories; and 1 gram of carbohydrate contains 4 calories. If you cut out fat, you end up eating far fewer calories; this is how most people go about attempting to lose weight. The problem is that carbohydrates and proteins influence blood sugar, while fats do not.

The glycemic index (GI) indicates how much impact foods have on blood sugar, and it is an important factor in your ability to maintain a healthy weight. The more fluctuations in blood sugar there are, the more insulin is produced and the more energy is stored as fat. This is key because the role of insulin is basically to remove excess sugar from the bloodstream, open up the fat cells, and store energy for future use. Fat loss cannot occur as long as insulin is active—it's metabolically impossible.

Overweight and obese people tend to have a harder time losing weight than thin people because their insulin systems are skewed in an unfavorable way. They typically have much lower insulin sensitivity, which means that a lot of insulin is required to handle even a small rise in blood sugar. The more insulin the body needs to create and the longer that insulin is active, the harder it is to burn body fat. Even if calories are kept to a minimum, some people have chronically high blood sugar and are in a permanent state of fat accumulation. In that situation, the body would rather slow down the metabolism than consume the extra fat.

Many factors other than food influence blood sugar levels, such as stress, caffeine, and poor sleep. I will look at these factors in more detail in later chapters, but it is important to adopt a holistic approach to health and to see the whole picture instead of zooming in on calories, carbs, or exercise. It's the totality of it all that brings results. The most important thing is to feel good while you are making the necessary lifestyle changes; otherwise it won't work.

A lot of people know about insulin and its role in blood sugar regulation, but few know about its counterpart, glucagon. Glucagon's role is the opposite of insulin's: glucagon allows the body to use stored fat for energy. The problem is that insulin and glucagon cannot be active at the same time. Even small amounts of carbohydrate can inhibit fat metabolism for hours. That's why some people believe that dieting is useless; no matter how few calories they consume, they still don't lose any weight. This is a painful situation in which to find oneself! However, the problem has nothing to do with discipline or the ability to endure hunger. Instead, it stems from the body's hormonal regulation system. A ketogenic diet allows you to bypass this system, lose weight, stay full, and cope with cravings much more efficiently.

COMPLEX CARBS AND INSULIN

Even foods with a low glycemic index and a low impact on blood sugar can trigger an insulin response. This includes complex carbs, fruits, nuts, seeds, and dairy products, which is why a simple low-carb or Paleo diet just won't cut it for some people.

Dairy products are an example of a group of foods with a low GI and a high insulin index. In addition to being addictive, they are insulinemic and can inhibit weight loss. Not everyone experiences this problem; it depends to some extent on how much and how frequently you eat dairy. But if you tend to overeat, avoid dairy.

Very lean protein, such as chicken, can also contribute to a small rise in insulin, which explains why every ketogenic meal should consist of a mix of proteins, fats, and vegetables. The fat helps lower the insulin response, because an important factor is the rate at which the carbs hit the bloodstream. When carbs enter the bloodstream more slowly, less insulin needs to be produced. This is why avocado is a keto-approved fruit despite its rather high carb content of 15 to 20 grams per fruit. Avocado consists of 80 percent healthy fats, and it's this high fat content that makes it ketogenic, because 60 to 80 percent fat is a perfect ratio for remaining in the ketogenic zone.

While you maintain this ratio, food cravings will cease to exist, and it will be easy to eat moderate portions, stay full longer, and have a steady stream of energy available throughout the day. Because it's a total match with the way the body is composed, you will have a chance to heal, lose weight, and get into naturally good shape without too much effort.

FUNDAMENTALS OF THE KETO DIET

- Ketogenic means a high ratio of fat in every meal, with 60 to 80 percent coming from natural sources. No fat needs to be added because the fat is already in the food.

- The ketogenic diet is suitable for long-term use because of its anti-inflammatory and healing properties. Regardless of whether you are fit, underweight, overweight, or obese, your body will find a balance and normalize in time.

- Ketogenic means that both protein and carbohydrate are kept to a minimum.

- Natural and unprocessed foods are the most important principle and should never be compromised. To achieve maximum health benefits, it's important to eat the foods that our bodies are designed to eat.

When people think of fatty foods, they typically picture greasy burgers, nachos, or French fries. The truth is that these processed foods are very high in carbs and have nothing in common with "real" fatty foods, such as eggs, meats, organ meats, seafood, fatty fish, butter, oils, and nuts. The difference is quite significant.

To wrap up this chapter, let me dispel some myths about the keto diet.

One of the most common misconceptions is that the keto diet is too nutrient-poor to be sustainable for a long time. The truth is that meats, organ meats, fish, poultry, eggs, animal fats, butter, coconut oil, leafy greens, and vegetables are incredibly nutrient-dense. Grains, pasta, and rice have almost no nutritional value.

Most fruits are not ketogenic because they are processed to such an extent that their natural vitamin and mineral content is almost completely wiped out. Today's fruits are genetically modified to appeal to our taste buds and have an unnaturally high fructose content.

Fiber from both fruits and grains is an issue for many people with stomach issues, such as IBS, because it can cause bloating, cramping, constipation, and diarrhea. Fructose can even influence food addictions and increase mood swings. Many people believe that fiber is important for normal bowel movements, but the truth is that fiber is rough on the gut lining and intestines. This means fiber is more likely to cause discomfort, constipation, and bloating. A diet that is naturally high in fat is the gentlest diet for a sensitive gut; a high-fat diet is also the fastest way to eliminate bloating and stomach discomfort. Many people who try a ketogenic diet are surprised at the positive effects it has on their gut health.

Another common misconception is that a keto diet is a high-calorie diet that focuses on eating huge amounts of fat. In reality, the natural fats already present in ketogenic foods are all you need; adding extra fat is unnecessary. If your brain is telling you that healthy, unprocessed foods are boring, you're hearing your food addictions talking, not your true nutritional needs.

Finally, it's important to realize that not all fats are good fats. A high fat ratio does not automatically qualify a diet as ketogenic. We will take a closer look at good and bad fats in Chapter 6, but first, we need to talk about the biochemistry behind fat loss and ketosis. This is where the fun starts!

CHAPTER 2

KETONES
and KETOSIS

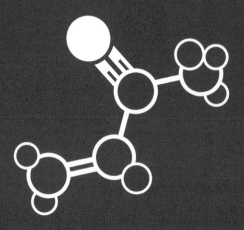

Let's jump right to the core of the ketogenic diet: ketosis itself! If you have ever experienced a state of ketosis, you might understand why I'm excited. If not, it will come as a happy surprise later. Ketosis is a nutritional state in which the body uses fat for fuel instead of glucose.

When we eat, the carbohydrate in that food is broken down and immediately used for energy. If there's no acute need for more energy, your body stores glucose in your liver and skeletal muscles in the form of glycogen. If the glycogen stores are full, surplus glucose is stored as fat. Glycogen stores are used as an energy source when the body needs more glucose than is readily available in the bloodstream—during exercise, for example. The body has a limited storage capacity for glycogen: about 2,000 calories. This limit is why carbohydrates are commonly referred to as the "limiting fuel" in physical performance.

Even on most low-carb and Paleo diets, people usually eat enough carbohydrates to hinder ketosis. The main focus of these diets is to maintain a stable blood sugar level, which is usually sufficient to reap many other health benefits, including weight loss. However, there is a whole new science to the different stages of ketosis. If you want to tap into the full range of human potential, I highly recommend experimenting with these metabolic advantages.

During ketosis, blood sugar is always low, regardless of how much food you are eating or whether you are fasting. Insulin is not active during ketosis, which means that no body fat is being stored. This is an ideal state when you are fully adapted to the ketogenic diet. It doesn't mean that you can't eat carbs ever again, but it does mean that your ability to switch between the two systems has increased dramatically. The fat-burning hormone, glucagon, is activated during ketosis, as one of its functions is to keep blood sugar levels in the normal range. Glucagon also works like a key to the fat cells, opening them up and inducing lipolysis, which is the breakdown of triglycerides into glycerol and free fatty acids. The body can use these molecules to fill most of its energy needs, but not all of them. That's why the body also needs to produce ketones.

Ketogenesis is the process by which ketone bodies are produced via the breakdown of fatty acids. Ketones are produced mainly in the mitochondria of liver cells when blood-borne glucose is unavailable or when fatty acids are available. Ketosis can occur only when carbohydrate intake is kept to a minimum or when glycogen reserves have been depleted after a hard workout. When the cells no longer use glucose, the body becomes fat-driven and runs on its own stored fat. This is very advantageous.

Vital organs, such as the heart and brain, don't run on fat, and therefore use ketones as their energy source. It might sound like a detour, but scientific evidence shows that both the brain and the heart function more effectively on ketones than they do on sugars. The liver also produces glucose from non-carbohydrate sources, such as pyruvate, lactate, glycerol, and glucogenic amino acids, in order to replenish the glycogen stores and normalize blood sugar. That means that even if you don't eat a single carb, you will still be able to use your glycogen stores and not have to worry about your blood sugar getting too low. This metabolic pathway is called gluconeogenesis, and even fatty acids can be converted to glucose via this process.

KETOSIS AND KETO-ACIDOSIS

During my initial experiments with ketosis, I was afraid of my ketones getting too high and inducing a state of ketoacidosis, which is potentially fatal. When my ketones went up, I usually ate some protein or even complex carbs to lower them. Now I know that ketoacidosis cannot occur in a person who has not been diagnosed with type 1 diabetes. When a type 1 diabetic suffers a biological stress event or fails to administer enough insulin, the liver cells might increase the metabolism of fatty acids into ketones in an attempt to supply energy to cells that are unable to transport glucose in the absence of insulin. The resulting high levels of blood glucose and ketone bodies lower the pH of the blood and trigger the kidneys to excrete the glucose and ketones. This is called osmotic diuresis, and it causes the removal of water and electrolytes from the blood, resulting in dangerous dehydration, tachycardia (rapid heart rate), and hypotension (low blood sugar).

Very rarely, ketoacidosis can also be seen in type 2 diabetics whose blood glucose levels have been very high for a significant period of time. People who suffer from this condition follow a very-high-carb diet that induces a state of glucose toxicity. This toxicity causes insulin production to cease, creating a temporary state physiologically similar to type 1 diabetes in which ketoacidosis can occur. Long-term alcoholics also can suffer from this phenomenon.

When people follow a low-carbohydrate diet and develop ketosis, it is a type of nutritional ketosis in which ketone concentrations are between 0.5 and 5 mmol, whereas pathological ketoacidosis is between 15 and 25 mmol. This higher range is simply not attainable by eating a low-carb diet, no matter how ketogenic it is.

FOOD AND ITS EFFECT ON KETOSIS

The three main macronutrients are fat, protein, and carbohydrate. These three nutrients have different effects on ketosis from their digestion, and consequently have different effects on blood glucose and hormones.

Fat is 90 percent ketogenic and 10 percent anti-ketogenic because of the small amount of glucose that is released in the conversion of triglycerides.

Protein is about 46 percent ketogenic and 54 percent anti-ketogenic because more than half of the ingested protein is converted to glucose, causing insulin levels to rise. The amount by which insulin is raised depends on the source and amount of the protein. Dairy foods, for example, are more insulinemic than beef or pork, and poultry is more insulinemic than fatty fish.

Carbohydrate is 100 percent anti-ketogenic because it raises blood levels of both glucose and insulin, even those carbohydrates found in whole grains, dark breads, bulgur, and brown rice.

Protein and carbohydrate prevent our bodies from transitioning into ketosis. The most important thing to understand is how our metabolic pathways use these nutrients for energy after we ingest them.

METABOLIC PATHWAYS

Human beings have three metabolic states: fed, fasting, and starving. Fed happens right after a full meal. Fasting occurs when we haven't eaten in more than eight hours. Starving is what we are when we haven't eaten in more than twenty-four hours.

In the fed state, nutrients are broken down into separate metabolic pathways. Fats go straight to the liver to be broken down into fatty acids and glycerol. The body then uses them to repair cells and produce important hormones, such as estrogen and testosterone. That is why a low-fat diet accelerates aging, because not enough fats are being consumed for cellular repair or the production of sex hormones.

Proteins are broken down into amino acids, which are used to synthesize muscles or repair tissues or stored as glucose. Carbohydrates are broken down into glucose, which causes an immediate spike in insulin, making it possible to store the glucose as either glycogen or fat in the fat cells. Carbohydrates can also be used for immediate energy.

When you haven't eaten in a few hours—preferably when you wake up in the morning and haven't eaten in eight to twelve hours (depending on when you had your last meal)—insulin is generally low and glucagon is activated. This means that your body is breaking down body fat for fuel. Liver glycogen is released to increase glucose levels in the bloodstream, and your brain is using this glucose as its energy source. The longer you remain in this fasted state, the more likely your liver is to start producing ketones, which is why fasting is quite an efficient way to reach ketosis.

After prolonged fasting, you reach a starved state. Exactly when starvation will occur differs from person to person: some might be able to fast for forty-eight hours before going into starvation, and for others it might take just twenty-four hours. When the body transitions into a starved state, the stored glycogen in the muscles and liver runs out, and the liver begins to break down lactate in order to create more glucose to fuel the red blood cells. Ketones are being produced and are detectable in the bloodstream, and the brain and muscles begin to use them as fuel through oxidization.

With the lack of glucose in your system, your body is essentially mimicking a state of starvation. That means, metabolically speaking, ketosis and starvation are the same thing. The only difference is that to enter and maintain a state of ketosis, you never need to starve yourself. As long as you keep your fat intake high, protein intake low, and carbohydrate intake to a minimum, there is no need to count calories or go hungry. Your body will simply burn fat and keep your energy and blood sugar levels stable without you needing to interfere with the process.

PROTEIN

Protein is a vital nutrient, but it's a bit tricky, because protein is 46 percent ketogenic and 54 percent anti-ketogenic, meaning that too much protein will knock you out of ketosis. You need to keep your protein intake within quite a narrow range to keep or build muscle mass and to maintain fat as your primary source of fuel.

However, eating ketogenic for a while becomes very natural, and there is no need to measure or count macronutrients (or "macros") to get it right. As a general rule, the more you exercise, the more protein you can consume without side effects, because glycogen depletion will allow both sugars and protein to be used up more quickly. That being the case, suggested protein intake depends on your lean body mass and your activity level.

- **Sedentary:** 1 gram of protein per kilogram of lean body mass
- **Lightly active:** 1 to 2 grams of protein per kilogram of lean body mass
- **Highly active:** 2 to 2.5 grams of protein per kilogram of lean body mass

GLUCOGENIC AMINO ACIDS

A glucogenic amino acid is an amino acid that can be converted into glucose via gluconeogenesis. This is in contrast to ketogenic amino acids, which are converted to ketone bodies. Only leucin and lysine are ketogenic. I will discuss these amino acids in more detail in Chapter 8, where you'll learn about protein and supplements.

FATS

Your fat intake determines how much of your body fat is used for fuel. Because fat is 90 percent ketogenic and only 10 percent anti-ketogenic, you can get away with eating large amounts of it. Even if glycerol from triglycerides produces glucose, it produces so small an amount that it will not negatively influence ketosis. Your body will use that glucose very efficiently, especially because fat is generally consumed over an entire day and not in a single sitting. The only time you should deviate from a consistent fat intake is after a workout. Eating fat after exercise is generally not recommended because it slows the process of digestion and slows the absorption of protein.

CARBO-HYDRATES

As one of the most restricted nutrients on a ketogenic diet, carbohydrate has the biggest effect on ketosis. The general rule is to consume no more than 20 grams of carbs a day to maintain ketosis. When your body breaks down carbohydrates and they enter your bloodstream, they are converted almost gram for gram to glucose. There, glucose can be burned up immediately for fuel, stored as glycogen in the muscles or liver, or, if excess carbohydrates are consumed, stored in fat cells.

In Chapter 10, I will discuss the use of carbohydrates on a ketogenic diet and the benefits carbs can have during workouts.

THE DIFFERENT TYPES OF KETONES

The body produces different types of ketones. Each of them is measured differently and indicates different things. The three endogenous ketone bodies are acetone, acetoacetic acid (AcAc), and β-hydroxybutyrate (BHB). AcAc is a ketone that can be converted by the liver into β-hydroxybutyrate or can spontaneously turn into acetone.

Acetone can be detected in the breath with a breath analyzer. AcAc can be detected in the urine with test strips that change color when ketones are present. BHB is found in the blood, behaving like an energy buffer that can be converted into AcAc and oxidized into energy.

Measuring ketones might seem like a tedious task, but it's a wonderful way to learn about your body and how different types of food affect it. A fair number of foods will influence your ability to burn fat, including almost all dairy foods, berries, nuts, dark chocolate, wine, and other spirits. Tolerance of these types of foods varies from individual to individual. Measuring ketones makes it easy to know whether you should exclude any foods for optimal results.

Personally, my state of ketosis is greatly affected by artificial sweeteners and substitute products like almond flour and coconut flour. I can have a glass of red wine now and then, but I can't indulge in nuts or chocolate (not even chocolate with a super-high cacao content). You don't have to be in ketosis all the time to feel great, lose weight, and heal your body, but it's good to know about the foods that might hinder your ability to burn fat.

HOW TO MEASURE YOUR KETONES

Urine test strips can be found at almost any drugstore and are fairly cheap. The color of the strip ranges from white to deep purple, with the darkest color indicating high levels of AcAc. Using these strips is the best and fastest way to know whether you are eating correctly and burning fat, especially if you are a beginner. After a while, your body's ability to use ketones as fuel will increase, which will lead to less accumulation of ketones in your kidneys and urine.

Blood ketone measuring devices are also available in most pharmacies, but they are a bit more expensive. Every test requires a small drop of blood, so you need to prick your finger, but the benefit is a more accurate reading, and you can measure your blood glucose with the same device. The blood sugar test strips are usually much cheaper than the blood ketone test strips. In the next chapter, I will talk about how to use blood glucose as a measure of ketosis.

A breath analyzer has the advantage of being reusable because it is just a mouthpiece connected to a sophisticated electronic acetone detector. You blow into the mouthpiece, and the breath analyzer blinks blue, green, yellow, or red. Red indicates a strong state of ketosis, which is optimal. You can find these analyzers online and at various other places. Although they are fairly expensive, breath analyzers do give quite accurate measurements.

Table 1 describes the readings you might get from the different devices and how to interpret them.

TABLE 1:
KETONE MEASUREMENTS AND RESULTS

Urine sticks (AcAc)	Blood ketone device (BHB)	Breath analyzer (acetone)	Result
White	<0.5 mmol/l	Blue	No ketosis
Pink	>0.5 mmol/l	Green	Nutritional ketosis
Purple	1 mmol/l	Yellow	Moderate ketosis
	1.5–3 mmol/l	Red	Optimal ketosis
	>3 mmol/l		Starvation
	>10 mmol/l		Ketoacidosis

Optimal ketosis is an ideal flow of energy to both brain and muscles, but not everyone prefers to be in a highly ketogenic state. Some people prefer to switch between different states of ketosis, and that's fine, too.

Ketoacidosis implies higher blood ketone levels than are attainable with a ketogenic diet. As you can see in the table, there's a big difference between optimal ketosis and ketoacidosis. Starvational ketosis is a state in which blood ketones are hovering between 3 and 5 mmol/l, which means that fat loss is occurring at a rapid rate. It's often quite difficult to reach a state of starvational ketosis without actually starving for long periods, but it's not a dangerous metabolic state to be in. It might occur naturally from time to time if you are a marathon runner or engage in a high-intensity sport for several hours, as it really speeds up ketone production. If ketones go up "too high" and you feel uncomfortable, the quickest remedy is to refuel your body with healthy and natural foods such as meat, fish, eggs, vegetables, and healthy fats. Even strictly ketogenic foods will lower your ketones as your body starts to rest and digest.

WHAT'S YOUR FAVORITE KETO ZONE?

Different people prefer different ketogenic states, depending on physical health, activity level, and food preferences. I always encourage people to experiment and find their own sweet spot when it comes to physical energy, mood, and weight loss. A higher state of ketosis is not necessarily better than a lower state; it all depends on what's working for you.

I personally enjoy a strict ketogenic diet with high ketones because it fuels my active lifestyle. If you are an athlete looking to optimize performance, high ketones really improve endurance. Less-active people might experience nervousness while in a highly ketogenic state and might not need the same flow of energy.

The ability to reach a state of ketosis differs from person to person. Some people go into ketosis easily, while others have blood sugar issues that obstruct both fat loss and ketosis. If you are under a lot of stress, are experiencing menopausal symptoms, are overweight, or have a hormonal issue, your body can produce a lot of blood sugar even if you don't eat a single carb. I will talk more about this topic in the next chapter.

CHAPTER 3

KETO ADAPTATION
and
BLOOD SUGAR

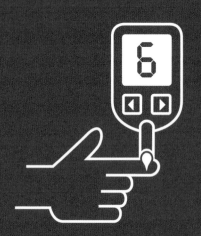

When you shift your diet toward more natural and unprocessed foods, you will begin to feel different. If you are attentive enough to your body's signals, you can almost tell when you have entered a state of ketosis. Hunger is severely diminished and energy levels increase. The need for sleep, rest, and snacking is greatly reduced.

If you have a food addiction or food allergies or you have been eating refined sugars, grains, and starch for a long time, your body might start to detox. This means that it begins healing, which can be quite uncomfortable for you. You might feel weak and tired for a couple of weeks as vital energy that is usually used by your muscles migrates to your inner organs to begin a process of rejuvenation and reconstruction.

The bile, intestines, arteries, veins, and capillaries declutter, flushing out medical waste, pollutants, heavy metals, and preservatives. Sometimes the body tries to get rid of everything at once but does not have the capacity to do so. That's why a toxic load can lead to rash, fever, eczema, lethargy, nervousness, depression, diarrhea, or constipation. It might seem odd that a truly healthy diet can induce such symptoms. However, these symptoms are signs of greater activity and "aliveness" as your body is beginning to heal itself from the inside.

It is important to understand that detoxing is about so much more than green juices and supplements from the pharmacy or health food store. These sorts of efforts to detox usually have little effect, if any at all. I watched my body heal with peace of mind because I was well prepared and knew the facts about what was happening to me. Without this understanding, it's easy to question the keto diet and find excuses to revert to old, destructive food choices.

During this transition period, please don't look for replacements for what you used to eat. Don't buy low-carb bread or sugar-free chocolate. Stick to meat, fish, eggs, poultry, vegetables, and animal fats. Keep it simple!

KETO-ADAPTATION

Some lucky people don't go through any detoxification process at all when they start a keto diet, but everyone needs to keto-adapt. It can take anywhere from a couple of weeks to a couple of months to do so successfully. Being keto-adapted means that there's no doubt about fat being the primary fuel for your body and glycogen stores acting as a backup only during intense exercise. This is the way we humans are naturally wired, and it's why a ketogenic diet helps us feel so much better, greatly enhancing our mental and physical performance.

The most important thing you can do to speed up the process of keto-adaptation is to be consistent and stick to the diet every day. No exceptions!

YOUR ADRENAL GLANDS

These days, many people have severe issues with their adrenal glands. These glands are found on top of the kidneys and produce a wide range of hormones that help regulate blood pressure, metabolism, and the immune system. They also influence the thyroid gland, which is one of the largest endocrine glands in the body. The thyroid is found in the neck and controls your metabolic rate. Imbalance in the adrenal system can cause a lot of things in your body to go haywire at the same time.

The adrenal glands produce the stress hormone cortisol. Most people suffer from inverted cortisol, which means that levels are high in the evening and low in the morning. Inverted cortisol leads to difficulties both sleeping and waking. Before I started my keto diet, I felt as though I was constantly sleep-deprived because my stressful university life coupled with my destructive diet caused me to suffer from this imbalance. It's like living in a fog that never lifts. Large amounts of sugar and stimulants seem to be the only things that wake you up.

This is why you should consider limiting your caffeine intake or even eliminating caffeine altogether. A cup of coffee here and there might be okay, but energy drinks and highly caffeinated supplements do more harm than good.

Cortisol can be measured in body fluids, such as urine, saliva, or blood. The amount of free cortisol in those fluids can be measured, but so can cortisone, its inactive form, or the metabolites that are the result of enzyme action. The ratios of any of these to the others also can be measured. These measurements have a diurnal rhythm, being higher and lower at different times of the day. Testing your cortisol levels either in a lab or with a saliva test kit at home can be very interesting.

Metabolic syndrome is a terrible and prevalent problem. It is the cluster of symptoms most strongly identified with diabetes: excess abdominal fat, high blood sugar, and a particular cholesterol profile. Metabolic syndrome is also linked to other potentially life-threatening conditions, such as heart disease and cancer. Even though a ketogenic diet is metabolically related to starvation, it places no stress on the adrenal glands. Instead, ketosis improves your cortisol profile.

KETOSIS AND GLUCOSE METABOLISM

Human beings have a very well developed glucose metabolism, which enables us to survive all the refined carbs that we are bombarded with. The problem is that this system is poorly adapted to continuous blood sugar spikes, which is why diabetes and obesity are so common.

At the beginning of human history, almost all foods were low in both energy and carbohydrates, which made insulin a crucial hormone to help the body store as much fat and nutrients as possible to increase the chances of survival. Some animals actually develop temporary diabetes during a food shortage because of this phenomenon.

Primal humans needed to be able to handle starvation while maintaining sufficient energy to find food or fend off threats. It was crucial to retain as much muscle mass as possible, despite limited food intake. Maintaining muscle is possible in ketosis because it's the most muscle-saving type of metabolism there is. There's no need to worry about losing muscle while you are losing weight on a keto diet.

If you are glucose-dependent and in a state of starvation, your body will break down muscle tissue to free amino acids and produce blood glucose. This phenomenon makes going on a low-calorie diet quite destructive because muscle tissue is broken down continuously. The lost weight consists of muscle, fat, and some water. Some well-known diets use ketosis to counteract this effect. The VLCD (very-low-calorie diet), which allows women 600 calories a day and men 700 calories a day, is the upper limit for the state of starvation. However, these methods can be quite painful and are unnecessary. A ketogenic diet induces the same metabolic state without deprivation or hunger. Ketosis is hormonal weight loss, which is the intelligent way to lose weight.

THE CALORIE MYTH

Energy from different food sources will have different effects on the body, even if the number of calories is the same. Fructose, modified starch, and high-fructose corn syrup are examples of substances that interfere with your body's regulatory and signaling systems. These substances hijack your brain, generate intense cravings, and cause feelings of hunger even if you are already full. They cause you to eat a lot more than you need to, which increases your body's ability to store fat. Many processed and unnatural foods have this effect, while natural and unprocessed foods do not.

Counting calories ignores too many important aspects of food, such as whether it makes you sick or fat or is addictive. Eating a calorie-restricted diet full of carbs, grains, and dairy products is a very uncomfortable business, because these foods manipulate your brain's reward circuits and thereby cause you to feel hungry and deprived.

When you follow a ketogenic diet, you eat only food that your body can recognize as food, which helps you feel satisfied with what you've consumed. Your body knows what it wants and how much it needs, and a ketogenic diet is all about tuning in to these inherent signaling systems. Counting calories interferes with your body's own intelligence, and you don't want to do that.

BLOOD SUGAR AND KETOSIS

One way to determine whether you have successfully keto-adapted is to check your blood sugar regularly. If you have an adrenal problem, you likely suffer from hyperglycemia, because stress causes the body to produce more glucose, which in turn affects blood sugar.

If your blood sugar is too high, you will not be able to keto-adapt. That is why it's so important to give yourself time to heal and not try to rush the process. Don't be too focused on weight loss, because weight loss cannot occur if everything else is out of balance.

A fasting glucose level higher than 6 mmol/l (110 mg/dl) might be an indicator of stress. Consider trying to eliminate other stressors, in addition to processed foods, from your life. Examples of stressors are too much blue light (in the form of computers, tablets, smartphones, and TV) before going to sleep, toxic relationships, negative working environments, and insufficient exercise. A sedentary lifestyle can be very stressful because our bodies are designed for movement.

Smoking and drinking alcohol, of course, will interfere enormously with your ability to feel good and maintain a healthy and vibrant body.

A clear sign of your adrenals healing is that your blood glucose is hovering around 4.5 mmol/l (60 mg/dl). This is also a notification that your body can produce ketones and begin burning body fat effortlessly. Achieving ketosis might require some serious effort on your part, though it will be easier if you are physically active.

CHAPTER 4

FAT *and* CHOLESTEROL

> " *There has never been solid evidence for the idea that saturated fats cause disease. We only believe this to be the case because nutrition policy has been derailed over the past half-century by a mixture of personal ambition, bad science, politics, and bias.* "
>
> **—NINA TEICHOLZ**,
> author of *The Big Fat Surprise*

Just as the body has requirements for cholesterol, it also needs saturated fat to function properly. One way to understand this is to consider the types of foods human beings consumed during their evolution. According to anthropologists, humans have eaten animal products for most of our existence. To suddenly suggest that saturated fats are harmful to us makes no sense—especially not from an evolutionary perspective.

As recently as 2010, the recommendations from the U.S. Department of Agriculture called for reducing saturated fat intake to a mere 10 percent or less of total calories—which is quite the opposite of what most people require for optimal health. The latest science suggests that healthy fats— saturated and unsaturated fats from whole food, animal, and plant sources—should comprise anywhere from 50 to 85 percent of total calorie intake. Saturated fats provide a number of important health benefits, including the following:

- They are building blocks for cell membranes, hormones, and hormone-like substances.

- They promote mineral absorption and conversion.

- They are carriers of important vitamins and anti-viral agents.

- They are optimal fuel for the heart and brain.

Worries about fat, cholesterol, and clogged arteries inhibit many people from reaping all the benefits of a ketogenic diet. Without sufficient fat intake, ketosis and keto-adaptation cannot be achieved. Fats are the foundation of a keto diet, and the belief that natural fats are somewhat dangerous does not go hand in hand with optimal health. When I started my keto journey, I was terrified of fat, like most people are. I was afraid that I would gain weight uncontrollably and have a heart attack in my sleep. It was several months before I dared to try heavy cream, crème fraîche, and butter, which allowed me to go deeper into ketosis. I was amazed to see that these foods didn't make me fat at all, but rather made me feel more satisfied while eating less. Heavy cream and crème fraîche are not the best choices because of the insulinemic casein protein, but they do go well with a low-carb diet. We have indeed been wrongly advised to avoid saturated fats and dietary cholesterol, despite there being no evidence of harm.

On the contrary, reducing dietary cholesterol might actually increase our risk of cardiovascular disease because our bodies need adequate cholesterol to perform a number of critical functions. There is strong evidence that people whose cholesterol levels are driven too low, as is widely achieved by statin drugs, have a higher risk of heart attacks. Cholesterol is needed to interact with proteins inside the cells, help regulate protein pathways, and ensure adequate cell signaling. Low cholesterol levels might negatively affect your brain health, hormone levels, heart disease risk, and more.

THE CHOLESTEROL MYTH

If high-cholesterol and high-fat diets are not the cause of heart disease, then how did this massive misinformation campaign start? It began more than 100 years ago when a German pathologist named Rudolph Virchow developed the Cholesterol Theory. After studying arterial plaques in corpses, Virchow theorized that cholesterol in the blood led to the development of plaque in the arteries. Later, Russian scientist Nikolai Anichkov fed rabbits cholesterol derived from egg yolks and saw them develop atherosclerotic changes. The fact that rabbits are herbivores and don't naturally consume cholesterol was not taken into account. Based on this flawed science, the notion that cholesterol leads to plaque deposits in the arteries started to take hold. At this time, it was not known that the liver produces 75 percent of the body's cholesterol or that every single cell needs cholesterol to produce cell membranes.

After World War II, the mortality rate from infectious diseases dropped while the incidence of heart disease rose. Scientists were desperately seeking a medical explanation when American nutritionist Ancel Keys published a seminal paper that served as the basis of nearly all the initial scientific support for the Cholesterol Theory. He found a significant correlation between high cholesterol and mortality in heart disease. However, he tampered with the results by selectively analyzing information from only six countries rather than comparing all the data available from the twenty-two countries studied.

Keys excluded those countries that didn't fit the hypothesis, namely those that showed a low fat intake and a high incidence of heart disease. Also ignored were those countries that showed a correlation between a high fat intake and a low incidence of heart disease. If all twenty-two countries had been included in Keys' analysis, no correlation would have been found.

Keys' paper garnered a lot of media attention. The nutrition community readily accepted his hypothesis and encouraged people to decrease their intake of red meat, eggs, dairy products, and animal fats. The study found its way onto the cover of the *Time* magazine, and Keys became famous. Although other scientists found contradictory evidence—for example, a link between sugar and heart disease—the cholesterol hypothesis was already recognized.

In the mid-1980s, Keys published his second paper, the well-known *Seven Countries Study,* which argued that saturated fat caused high cholesterol and heart disease. Keys followed 12,000 middle-aged men for several years and recorded their diets and cholesterol levels. Keys then "proved" the correlation using unsound statistical methods and maneuvers.

The next major support for the Cholesterol Theory was the Framingham Heart Study, which is often cited as proof of the correlation between cholesterol and heart disease. This study began in 1948 and involved some 6,000 people from the town of Framingham, Massachusetts, who filled out detailed questionnaires about their lifestyle habits and diets. The study is credited with identifying heart disease risk factors such as smoking, high blood pressure, lack of exercise, and high cholesterol. The cholesterol link was weak because researchers noted that those who weighed more and had abnormally high blood cholesterol levels were slightly more at risk for future heart disease, but the study was widely publicized nevertheless.

When a follow-up study done thirty years later showed that high cholesterol wasn't a risk factor for men older than 47 or for women of any age, it got little attention. By that time, cholesterol-lowering medications were not only a billion-dollar industry, but the most profitable category of medicine in the world. In fact, more men whose cholesterol has been declining over the years eventually die of heart disease. Many subsequent studies have supported the theory that there is no correlation between blood cholesterol and heart disease. On the contrary, patients who have suffered a heart attack often have significantly lower cholesterol levels than healthy people the same age.

It is obvious that media attention, prestige, and profit are behind the fact that this misinformation has persisted for so long, even though the myth about saturated fat and cholesterol continues to fall apart as a steady stream of new books and studies on the topic are being published.

So what *does* cause atherosclerosis?

Atherosclerosis is caused by oxidized lipoproteins penetrating the arterial wall, which incites inflammation and damages the arterial tissue. Atherosclerosis is *not* caused by fat attaching itself to the insides of the arteries like cooking fat in a kitchen pipe. Inflammation generally is caused by a high intake of processed foods, refined sugars, starches, and grains, as well as environmental toxins and alcohol consumption. Inflammation has nothing to do with dietary cholesterol.

A CRASH COURSE IN CHOLESTEROL

Cholesterol is a waxy lipid found in every cell membrane and in blood plasma. Its jobs include insulating neurons, building and maintaining cell membranes, metabolizing fat-soluble vitamins, producing bile, and kick-starting the body's synthesis of many hormones, including sex hormones.

Given all the work cholesterol must do, the liver is careful to ensure that the body always has enough cholesterol, producing about 1,000 to 1,400 milligrams every day. In comparison, the recommended limit of 300 milligrams of dietary cholesterol is a drop in the bucket. The liver has sophisticated feedback mechanisms that regulate cholesterol production in response to dietary intake. When you eat more cholesterol, your liver manufactures less of it, and when you eat less, it makes more. Dietary cholesterol doesn't even affect total blood cholesterol. In fact, when you do eat cholesterol, your body simply makes less to keep your blood levels in balance.

Blood is water-soluble and fat is fat-soluble. Therefore, fat needs to be transported by lipoproteins (spherical fat particles with water-soluble proteins around their exteriors) in the bloodstream. These lipoproteins are divided by size. VLDL (very-low-density lipoproteins, calculated by measuring triglycerides) is the largest. LDL (low-density lipoproteins) and HDL (high-density lipoproteins) are the smallest. When you go to the doctor for a cholesterol test, you will get these three values, as well as a total value.

Fat and cholesterol from food ends up in the liver and is packaged as VLDL, which travels the bloodstream and is distributed to cells and tissues. As the cells absorb more fat and cholesterol, VLDL particles shrink and turn into smaller LDL particles. Sometimes a whole LDL particle is absorbed by a cell if that cell needs more building blocks. LDL is called "bad" cholesterol because it's the particle that is found in the walls of damaged blood vessels, but it's really not bad. On the contrary, the latest science shows that there is no bad cholesterol. LDL has been wrongly accused of a crime it didn't commit!

Eating naturally saturated fats increases HDL cholesterol, while eating carbohydrates lowers HDL cholesterol. HDL is the so-called "good" cholesterol because all it does is transport excess cholesterol particles back to the liver to be broken down. The liver then excretes the cholesterol particles through bile. HDL naturally helps get rid of excess cholesterol when the body is finished with it.

The latest research on LDL shows that there are subcategories of this cholesterol transporter and that some are more dangerous than others. The larger LDL particles are now thought to play little or no significant role in heart disease. On the other hand, the smaller, denser LDL particles are believed to be most involved in the inflammation that begins the atherosclerosis cascade. Small LDL particles are promoted by a diet high in simple carbs. Ironically, it's not the cholesterol part of LDL or HDL that is dangerous, but the actual lipoprotein. Unfortunately, once medicine found a way to differentiate between the amounts of HDL and LDL in a cost-effective blood test, the cholesterol part got the short end of the deal.

Each VLDL and LDL particle has another protein bound to it: Apolipoprotein B, or ApoB for short. By measuring ApoB, it's possible to detect even the smallest particles. However, these measurements don't say anything about the ratio of large to small particles; they merely detect LDL particles, regardless of size. To make predictions about heart disease, you need to know the ratio of LDL to HDL. You want this ratio to be as low as possible—in other words, you want more HDL than LDL. More HDL ensures that all excess LDL is captured and transported back to the liver.

Because HDL is bound to Apolipoprotein A1 (ApoA1), the ApoA1 test can show the exact HDL figure. By dividing ApoB by ApoA1 (ApoB/ApoA1), you can get a better reading and risk assessment.

MEASURING CHOLESTEROL

Right now, millions of people around the world are taking cholesterol-lowering drugs without needing them and unnecessarily suffering the risk of serious side effects. Total cholesterol and LDL cholesterol levels are poor markers of heart disease risk, but many people are being unnecessarily medicated because doctors tend to focus on these numbers.

There's no reason for healthy people to measure their cholesterol levels, but if you are starting a ketogenic diet and are curious about cholesterol, feel free to go ahead and take the test.

Total cholesterol is the sum of all particles and should be below 5.5 mmol/l, although most people have a higher value. Most people who are on a long-term ketogenic diet have values around or above 7 mmol/l. Especially for women, high total cholesterol indicates a decreased risk of heart disease and neurological decline.

Triglycerides should be under 1.7 mmol/l. A figure higher than 1.7 could be a sign of metabolic syndrome and associated increased health risks. High values are often attributable to a high carbohydrate intake. Ketogenic dieters usually hover around 0.2 to 0.7 mmol/l because of their low carbohydrate intake.

Fat takes the form of triglycerides when it travels to the body's tissues through the bloodstream. The relationship between triglycerides and cholesterol is more of an association. High triglyceride levels are fueled by a high-carb diet and are often a marker for insulin resistance and inflammation. High levels are often seen with low HDL cholesterol.

HDL is the "good" cholesterol, and it increases with a high intake of saturated fat. Men should not go below 1.0 mmol/l, and women shouldn't dip below 1.3 mmol/l. People with metabolic syndrome typically have very low levels of HDL. A low-carb enthusiast usually has amounts well beyond these, in the region of 1.3 to 2.5 mmol/l.

LDL is recommended to be below 3.0 mmol/l, though it's a bit difficult to interpret the value. Low triglycerides probably indicate that the LDL particles are large and fluffy, and high triglycerides that the LDL particles are small and dense. An LDL level between 3 and 4 mmol/l is fine while in ketosis.

ApoB/ApoA1 ratio is the most modern cholesterol test because it measures the amounts of HDL and LDL particles and calculates the ratio between the two. A low value is good; it is recommended that this value should be below 0.9 for men and below 0.8 for women. People who follow a ketogenic diet are usually well beyond these numbers.

CHOLESTEROL AND INFLAMMATION

In response to an inflammatory situation, the body uses cholesterol as a "bandage" to temporarily cover any lesion in the arterial wall. If the inflammation is resolved, the bandage goes away and repair occurs, without causing any harm. Unfortunately, in most cases, the inflammation isn't resolved. The cholesterol plaque is eventually acted upon by macrophages and oxidized to a point where it takes up more space in the artery, slows arterial flow, and can eventually break loose to form a clot. It all boils down to inflammation as the number-one factor in many diseases, including heart disease. This is now proven, but it still gets little attention, and no real prevention or treatment takes place.

Many people check their cholesterol levels every five years or less but never check the biomarkers for inflammation, which are a lot more interesting.

Furthermore, nearly every study suggests that LDL is a threat only when it's oxidized. What oxidizes LDL? Free radicals, mostly caused by trans fats, food additives, and environmental toxins. Free radicals are counteracted by antioxidants from vegetables, nuts, oils, and berries.

So substantially elevated cholesterol, low HDL, or high LDL might be reason to reconsider your lifestyle, as your body might be trying to tell you that something is amiss. However, elevated cholesterol is a symptom rather than the main issue, because cholesterol profiles are affected by other conditions, such as untreated diabetes, pre-diabetes, heart disease (a symptom, not a cause), hypothyroidism, stress, or liver conditions.

OTHER GOOD TESTS FOR MONITORING HEART HEALTH

1. HDL/Total cholesterol ratio

Divide your HDL level by your total cholesterol number. Ideally, the result should be above 0.24; a result below 0.1 is a significant indicator of heart disease risk.

2. Triglycerides/HDL ratio

Divide your triglyceride number by your HDL level. Ideally, the result should be below 2.

3. NMR lipoprofile

This might be the most powerful test for evaluating heart disease risk because it determines your proportion of the smaller and more damaging LDL particles. It also correlates to insulin and leptin resistance.

4. Fasting insulin

A normal fasting blood insulin level is below 5. However, the ideal level is below 3. If your insulin level is higher than 5, the most effective way to optimize it is to eliminate all refined sugars and processed grains.

5. Fasting blood glucose

A fasting blood glucose figure above 6 mmol/l indicates an increased risk of coronary artery disease. Ideally, your fasting blood glucose should be below 5 if you are keto-adapted or below 6 if you are not.

6. Waist-to-hip ratio

Visceral fat, the type of fat that collects around internal organs, is a well-recognized risk factor for heart disease. The simplest way to evaluate your risk is to measure your waist-to-hip ratio (see Table 2).

7. Iron level

Excess iron can increase oxidative stress and damage blood vessels. Serum ferritin levels should be below 80 ng/ml.

TABLE 2:
WAIST-TO-HIP RATIO

$$RATIO = \frac{WAIST}{HIPS}$$

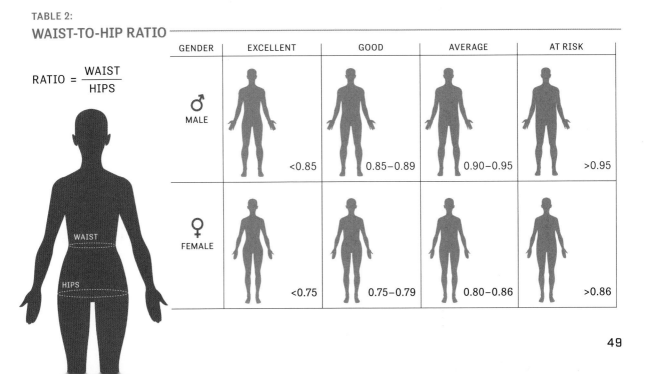

GENDER	EXCELLENT	GOOD	AVERAGE	AT RISK
♂ MALE	<0.85	0.85–0.89	0.90–0.95	>0.95
♀ FEMALE	<0.75	0.75–0.79	0.80–0.86	>0.86

HOW TO OPTIMIZE CHOLESTEROL LEVELS

First, if you are on cholesterol-lowering medication, consider quitting right away. Talk to a cardiologist or other doctor you trust and do your own research online. An extensive number of publications explain the negative effects of statins. It's widely known that lowering CoQ10 levels is a good way to lower cholesterol because CoQ10 and cholesterol are produced in the same way. Statins also reduce the blood cholesterol that transports CoQ10 and other fat-soluble antioxidants. The loss of CoQ10 leads to a loss of cell energy and increases free radicals; this increase in free radicals can further damage mitochondrial DNA, effectively triggering a vicious cycle of increasing free radicals and mitochondrial damage.

In the U.S., there are seldom official warnings regarding CoQ10 depletion from taking statin drugs, but labeling in Canada clearly warns of CoQ10 depletion and even notes that this nutrient deficiency "could lead to impaired cardiac function in patients with borderline congestive heart failure." As your body's store of CoQ10 gets further and further depleted, you might suffer from fatigue, muscle weakness and soreness, and eventually heart failure. All this means that it is imperative to take a CoQ10 supplement if you take statins. If you are over 40, you should take Ubiquinol (a reduced form of CoQ10).

The most effective way to optimize your cholesterol profile and prevent heart disease is via diet and exercise. Reducing cholesterol is quite simple, too. Remember that 75 percent of your body's cholesterol is produced by your liver, which is influenced by your insulin levels. Therefore, if you optimize your insulin levels, you will automatically and simultaneously optimize your cholesterol, reducing your risk of both diabetes and heart disease. There is no "magic pill" for preventing heart disease because the underlying cause is insulin resistance caused by eating too many sugars, grains, and especially fructose.

My primary recommendations for safely regulating cholesterol and reducing your risk of heart disease include the following:

- First and foremost, eliminate processed and industrialized foods and adopt a healthy, natural, low-carb diet. This will also reduce your risk of diabetes.

- Get plenty of high-quality animal-based omega-3 fats from fish and seafood. Don't consume plant-based omega-3, as our bodies can't process it.

- Reduce your consumption of damaging omega-6 fats, trans fats, and vegetable oils. The next chapter goes into more detail about good and bad fats.

- Include coconut, coconut oil, olive oil, eggs, avocados, and organic grass-fed meats in your diet.

- Optimize your vitamin D levels.

- Exercise daily.

- Avoid smoking and drinking alcohol.

- Get plenty of restorative sleep.

- Stay away from unnatural blue light late at night (typically from TVs and computers), which reduces melatonin production and, in turn, serotonin levels.

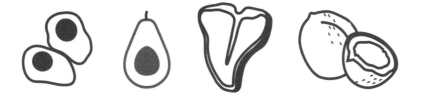

CHAPTER 5

GOOD FATS
and
BAD FATS

Isn't fat totally devoid of nutrients? How do you get your vitamins if you're eating all that fat? These are common questions for people who are considering a ketogenic diet. It's helpful to look at the health benefits of certain fatty foods. For instance, the richest source of natural vitamin E is red palm oil, while the richest source of choline is egg yolk. One of the better sources of vitamin K is butter, and the best dietary source of vitamin D is cod liver oil. Organ meats such as liver are extremely nutrient-dense and rich in vitamin C. Many generations of indigenous people, including the Tokelau, Masai, and Inuit, have existed solely on these types of foods. And let's not forget that saturated fat has been a healthy human staple for thousands of years.

The keto diet (or LCHF) might make it seem as if any type of fat is acceptable, but that isn't true. Most of the fats available today are unnatural and hazardous to our health. For example, vegetable fats such as canola oil, rapeseed oil, and sunflower oil are inflammatory and dangerous when consumed in large quantities. On the other hand, omega-3 fatty acids from fish lower inflammation and increase HDL cholesterol.

The industrialized fats found in processed foods and ready-made meals are not recognized by the body at all. And there are many fats that look like fats but are not, such as margarine. This chapter will help you distinguish these bad fats from the good ones that you should be consuming.

DANGEROUS FATS

The worst fats are polyunsaturated because they are reactive and easy to oxidize. Therefore, polyunsaturated fats contribute to destructive chemical chain reactions, such as lipid peroxidation. This means that reactive oxygen species, such as free radicals, attack the CH2-group between two double bonds and initiate an oxidation reaction. This is also known as oxidative stress, which is corrosive to cells and cell membranes. If you have a limited understanding of chemistry, don't worry. The take-home message is that polyunsaturated fats (such as canola and sunflower oil) are bad health choices because they cause premature cell aging. If your cells get old and sick, so do you!

Atoms that are missing an electron are likely to "steal" electrons from nearby stable atoms, which induces this dangerous chain reaction. If this happens with the atoms and molecules in the cell membrane, the membrane will break and be unable to function. If the cells in blood vessel walls can't function properly, arterial plaque and atherosclerosis can develop. Oxidized lipids and membrane damage are important factors in accelerated aging and age-related diseases.

The unnaturally high monounsaturated fat content in many industrialized foods stems from their inclusion of olive and canola oils. Vegetable and seed oils are also rich in inflammatory omega-6 fatty acids, which have negative effects on blood vessels. A little vegetable oil here and there is okay, but keep it to a minimum. Choose other oils instead whenever you can. Both avocado oil and coconut oil have better lipid profiles.

OMEGA-3 DIFFERS DEPENDING ON THE SOURCE

Omega-3 fatty acids have always had a good reputation among nutritionists and are generally regarded as a healthy choice. Their blood-thinning and anti-inflammatory properties soften the skin and hair, protect the brain, and increase fat metabolism. These are just a few of the positive aspects. However, bear in mind that a lot of foods that are high in omega-3 are not healthy.

Flaxseed oil is almost 50 percent omega-3, but when omega-3 fatty acids are vegetable-based, the human body cannot utilize them. Omega-3 fatty acids must be animal-based for our bodies to recognize and use them, because only animal-based omega-3 can be converted to other healthy fats within the omega-3 family, such as EPA and DHA. Vegetable-based omega-3 has a completely different chemical structure and can be just as reactive and inflammatory as omega-6 fatty acids (see below) in higher quantities.

Small amounts of vegetable-based omega-3 from walnuts and flax seeds are okay.

LIMIT OMEGA-6 AND OTHER BAD FATS

Omega-6 is a fatty acid that can cause inflammation, even in small portions. This is a good thing because inflammation is an important defense mechanism in the body. However, the human body needs only a small amount of omega-6, so we almost always consume it in excess, which triggers too much inflammation. Food producers use a lot of cheap, processed vegetable oils (containing omega-6) as additives and fillers in almost every type of food, from canned fish and meats to fried foods to powdered soups.

Some vegetable fats and margarines have added plant sterols to make them appear healthier because they interfere with the body's natural regulation of cholesterol. These fats are not healthy, though, because the body needs its cholesterol. Stay away from these hazardous fats.

Palm oil is a healthy oil, but the expansion of oil palm plantations is threatening rain forests and peat lands (swampy areas where soils are made up of decomposed vegetation). The peat lands act as a sponge, soaking up water and helping to prevent floods, as well as storing a large quantity of carbon. Palm oil plantations drain these peat lands and the stored carbon reacts with air, releasing carbon dioxide into the atmosphere, thereby increasing the concentration of greenhouse gases in the air.

LOW-FAT OR WHOLE-FAT?

There's nothing wrong with buying and liking low-fat products, as long as the manufacturer hasn't compensated for the lack of flavor by adding sugar. Some dairy products are naturally low in fat, which means that the higher-fat versions are actually more processed than the low-fat alternatives. One example is small curd cottage cheese, which is one of many popular dairy foods in northern Europe.

Most low-fat food manufacturers use chemical engineering to raise the water content of their products as much as possible. What you are paying for, then, is expensive water. If you prefer that watered-down taste, you can achieve it much cheaper at home. Just buy whole-fat products and mix them with water!

MODERN TYPES OF FAT

Cookies, chips, ready-made meals, powdered soups, and margarine often contain large quantities of artificially saturated fats. Unsaturated fats can be processed into saturated fats to give a product special qualities, like crispness, hardness, or a specific melting point. Unfortunately, a lot of trans fats are formed during this processing, and trans fats carry many negative health effects. The body doesn't have a blueprint of which types of fats it needs to build cell membranes and hormones; it simply uses the fats that are available. If these fats are highly unnatural, the body will not be able to utilize them correctly. For example, cell membranes that incorporate trans fats will not be able to signal properly, which can lead to serious genetic and metabolic diseases, such as cancer, in the long run. Trans fats have a very poor reputation and are said to increase the risk of heart disease, obesity, and type 2 diabetes.

To minimize the amount of trans fats in their food products, many food manufacturers use unethically sourced red palm oil or simply process the existing fats even further to get rid of the trans bonds chemically. Unfortunately, a double-processed fat is not healthier than a normally processed one. The only difference is that the food producer can now add a "No trans fats!" label to the product.

CHOOSING GOOD FATS

Choosing the right fats when you are on a high-fat diet is not a simple task, but once you know more about the different types of fats, you can make better choices in the supermarket.

In general, saturated fats are safer than polyunsaturated fats, and omega-3 from animal sources is preferable to omega-3 from plant-based sources.

Butter has a high proportion of saturated fat, provides a better mix of fats with a better lipid profile, and can withstand both heating and frying. Butter contains one-third monounsaturated and two-thirds saturated fat, which is similar to the fat ratio of a human being. Choosing the same types of fats that are naturally present in your body means that there will be no unpleasant side effects when they are broken down and utilized. They are also highly compatible with your own fat metabolism and therefore can increase your metabolic rate.

Coconut oil is a healthy oil that contains 60 percent MCTs (medium-chain triglycerides), which is a fatty acid that cannot be broken down in the gut and therefore goes straight to the bloodstream, where it is utilized for energy. Coconut oil also has widely recognized anti-inflammatory properties and can be ingested or used externally.

MCT oil can be purchased online or from most supplement stores, but be careful—it can be a little harsh on your stomach if you aren't used to eating a lot of fat. When you are keto-adapted, you will be able to use MCT oil to increase your metabolism, get rid of cravings, or gain extra energy during workouts. Before your body adapts to a high fat intake, you can supplement with ox bile, which helps you break down fat more efficiently until your body is able to do it smoothly on its own. Ox bile is available in pill form from health food and supplement stores.

Lard, duck fat, and other animal fats have become increasingly popular in recent years because they are perfect for cooking and frying. They are also ideal for a ketogenic diet.

Lastly, avoid margarine, which is one of the most heavily processed and unnatural products out there. This odorless, tasteless "fat" could just as well have been used for making paint or beauty products. What makes margarine look edible are the yellow food coloring and butter aroma added to it, but only after a string of refining processes that expose it to acids, lye, petroleum, and other chemicals. Choose butter instead. The milk fat in butter is a rich source of vitamin K, which is good for both heart health and metabolism.

ETHICAL AND ENVIRON-MENTAL CONCERNS

If possible, be mindful of the sources of your food products to make better health choices. Conscious food choices affect both your health and the environment long term, so the next time you are in the grocery store, take an extra look at the foods you are thinking of buying. Where do they come from? How long is the list of ingredients? Can you pronounce everything on that list?

Grain-fed cows are kept indoors and fed grain, which isn't what cows naturally eat. Studies show that the longer cattle are fed grain, the greater their fatty acid imbalance becomes. After 200 days on a feedlot, grain-fed cows have an omega-6 to omega-3 ratio that exceeds 20:1. Cattle are fed grain for 200 days or more in many countries. Because omega-6 is an inflammatory fatty acid, it's important to choose grass-fed meat and dairy over grain-fed whenever possible. Grass-fed beef is naturally leaner than grain-fed beef, and omega-3 in beef from cows that fed on grass is 7 percent of the total fat content, compared to 1 percent in beef from cows fed only grain. Grass-fed beef is also more nutrient-rich. If you can choose meat that is hormone- and antibiotic-free as well, you'll get health food of the highest order.

Pigs are also fed grain, as well as soy, bone meal, and other highly unnatural foods. This affects their fatty acid ratio in the same way it affects cows. There's also a great difference between pastured eggs—where the chickens get to eat vegetables, insects, and fresh green grass—and eggs from chickens that are fed a diet consisting solely of corn (which is what many egg-laying hens are fed). Standard supermarket eggs can have an omega-6 to omega-3 ratio of 20:1, compared to 1.5:1 in pastured eggs.

Palm oil is often confused with coconut oil, which is an ethically produced, healthy fat. In addition to deforestation caused by palm oil plantations (see page 55), oil palms have been found to have been sprayed with large amounts of pesticides. Toxic chemicals affect wildlife and the entire ecosystem. Recently, several organizations have begun trying to create a sustainable palm oil industry. The Green Palm logo certifies that a company supports sustainable palm oil. The Wetlands International organization works to improve areas that have been destroyed by the drainage of peat swamps. Some restoration/regeneration of the world's rain forests is still possible.

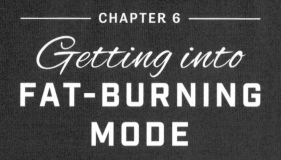

— CHAPTER 6 —

Getting into
FAT-BURNING
MODE

Now that you know a little bit about how your body works, it's time for you to begin your own keto journey. This chapter gives you some practical steps to follow. First, I will talk about transitioning into ketosis and what to do once you achieve ketosis. Then I will discuss how to distinguish true ketosis from "false" ketosis. Finally, I'll talk about the different aspects of weight loss.

LET'S GET STARTED!

If this is the first time you've tried to transition from being a carb-burner to being a fat-burner, you might find the process a bit challenging, but the longer you are in ketosis, the easier it will be to switch between these two fuels. You might not even want to switch back to burning carbs once you have found your ketogenic sweet spot.

You can transition into ketosis in several different ways, and I will walk you through each method. The most common method is to reduce your carb intake week by week until it reaches 20 grams a day or less. This should be accompanied by light workouts, as discussed in Chapter 9.

Depending on your fitness level, a light workout can involve bodyweight training, jogging, or walking. Skip heavy workouts or hours on the treadmill during this transition phase so that your cortisol levels can normalize and your body can find its pace in this new metabolic state. Light workouts will give you great long-term results, especially if you have adrenal problems or a slow thyroid.

However, some people get discouraged if they need to wait to see results from a method they aren't even sure is worth the effort. This is especially true when it comes to weight loss, particularly for those who have already had many failed attempts. I assure you that the ketogenic diet works very well for weight loss. However, I want you to remember that diet is just one small aspect. Keto is more of a lifestyle than anything else. I know I don't need to preach about ketosis because athletes and fitness enthusiasts use it from time to time to look their best for a competition or photo shoot. Of course, that approach is fine, too. Some people don't want to buy the whole package, but simply look good fast.

If you're one of those impatient people who want to see immediate results on the scale, I'm not going to try to talk you out of it. I want to give you the best methods for achieving your goal.

Let's get started!

FAT FASTING

First comes the very effective fat fast, which forces your body to use body fat rather than glucose for fuel. It usually generates about 11 lost pounds in a single week. Most of this weight is water, though some of the lost weight will come from fat, which can be quite motivating.

While fat fasting, you eat only pure fat or high-fat foods—nothing else. Basically, this means anything with a high fat content, little protein, and few carbs, such as butter, coconut oil, fried eggs, heavy cream, mayonnaise, fried salmon, and bacon. Wait until you're really hungry before you begin your fat fast, and make sure to eat only keto-approved foods. One deviation will spoil the whole process: a single piece of chocolate, a small piece of fruit, or even a splash of milk in your coffee. You cannot deviate one tiny bit because everything counts. You can't be a little bit in ketosis. Either you're in ketosis or you're not, which means that either you get results or you don't.

A couple years after I started keto, a lot of people were curious about my diet and workout routine, so I started blogging. I posted my thoughts and feelings about the ketogenic diet on my blog, and its popularity increased until it became one of the most visited health blogs in Sweden. My blog remains quite popular as interest in this lifestyle continues to grow. When I felt confident enough, I started coaching people who wanted to get into shape. I did this for about two years, which was enormously helpful for my understanding of the psychological aspects of eating habits and food addictions.

People told me that they wanted my help to get in shape and also wanted a meal plan to follow. I made individualized meal plans for every one of my clients to fit their goals and current conditions. Soon I saw that even though most people succeeded, a small percentage didn't. This piqued my interest, and I began to investigate how it was possible that my methods didn't work for all my clients. What I found was that people with a long-term, heavy food addiction continued to overeat and include foods that weren't on the plan. As it turned out, most of them didn't realize the impact of overindulgence—even on healthy foods—and didn't think that a small deviation would matter. The thing is that overindulging is bad for your entire system. Intense exercise or starvation cannot counteract overindulgence. If you continually overeat, you will get fat. If you continually overeat and compensate for it with starvation or strenuous exercise, you have an eating disorder.

Because fat is 90 percent ketogenic and 10 percent anti-ketogenic, a meal consisting of eggs, bacon, and butter will still generate a tiny amount of glucose, which is why it's unnecessary to gorge. Stay in contact with your body's internal signaling system and eat until you feel satisfied.

If you don't know the macronutrient distributions for different foods, read the labels or download an app for your phone to help you manage it. Don't do any guessing in the beginning, because many foods contain a lot of carbohydrates without tasting sweet at all. For example, ketchup, ready-cooked meats, and sausages contain lots of carbs and can really trip you up if you aren't careful.

CALORIE-RESTRICTED FAT FASTING

If you really don't know when you are hungry or full and need some guidance in the beginning, try a calorie-restricted fat fast. It's inspired by the Atkins diet and includes five tiny meals per day, each providing 200 calories.

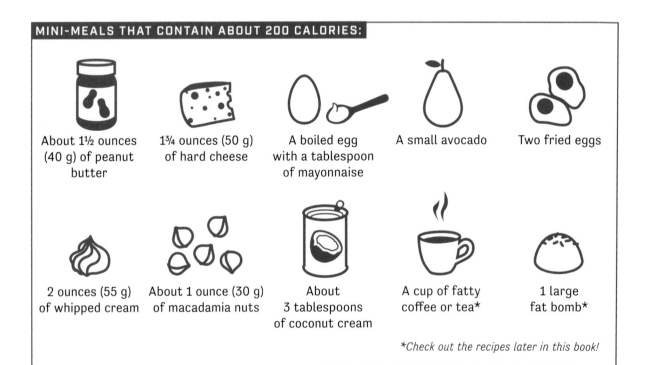

MINI-MEALS THAT CONTAIN ABOUT 200 CALORIES:

About 1½ ounces (40 g) of peanut butter

1¾ ounces (50 g) of hard cheese

A boiled egg with a tablespoon of mayonnaise

A small avocado

Two fried eggs

2 ounces (55 g) of whipped cream

About 1 ounce (30 g) of macadamia nuts

About 3 tablespoons of coconut cream

A cup of fatty coffee or tea*

1 large fat bomb*

Check out the recipes later in this book!

These are just a few examples, and I'm sure you can find even more 200-calorie mini-meals. Fatty coffee, cheese, and whipped cream are not 100 percent keto-approved, but they can be okay during the transition period. Most people don't want to go cold turkey on everything, but prefer to start with a more flexible approach. You can phase things out at your own pace. If you like, have a treat here and there as long as doing so suits your lifestyle.

I recommend doing a calorie-restricted fat fast or a normal fat fast (see page 63) for a week and seeing what happens. Monitor your body's reactions closely and buy urine test strips at the drugstore to detect ketones in your urine. After several years on the keto diet, I no longer use the urine test strips because my body has learned to use ketones efficiently. For a beginner, though, these strips can be quite helpful. Plus, they're cheap and easy to use!

CLASSIC FASTING

Fasting is a way of rebooting both your immune system and your food preferences. After a fast, you are much more likely to choose healthy foods than unhealthy ones, and you are more likely to eat moderate amounts. If you haven't tried fasting before, I strongly suggest that you try an eight-hour fast to start and then increase the duration to twelve or sixteen hours. Some people like to fast once a month for twenty-four hours, or even longer. It's up to you. If you have a severe medical condition or you take prescription medicine, consult with your doctor first, especially if you take medication to regulate your blood sugar.

Fasting is a way to get your body to produce ketones, and it takes between twenty-four and forty-eight hours. It is possible to fast your way into ketosis, and fasting is probably one of the fastest ways to achieve ketosis. You also can do a combination of classic fasting and either fat fasting or calorie-restricted fat fasting. The focus of the first week is to see traceable ketones in your urine, blood, or breath, which gives you a quick understanding of what it's all about.

The benefit of reaching a state of ketosis fairly quickly is to experience the dramatic difference between carb-burning and fat-burning. Decreased hunger and cravings and rapid weight loss are quite motivating for most people.

KETOSIS BY TRAINING

If you are already quite fit, have healthy adrenal glands, and are used to hard daily workouts, reaching a state of ketosis will be easy for you. Just do your normal workout, whether it's running, weight lifting, or a sport, and focus on emptying your glycogen reserves. That might mean that you need to do a longer or more intense workout than normal, but when you feel like you have "hit the wall," you're done.

If you usually have a protein shake and some carbs after your workout, feed your muscles some fat instead. Appropriate choices include high-fat foods such as eggs, butter, fatty fish, bacon, and ground pork or beef with heavy cream. Be careful with protein, which might impede your transition into ketosis. If you aren't hungry, skip eating altogether until you feel really hungry. Don't worry about your muscles; they won't disappear overnight.

WHEN YOU ARE IN KETOSIS

When you begin to detect ketones in your urine, blood, or breath, you can start to include more vegetables in your diet and experiment with different types of foods. You still don't need hard workouts because you are not keto-adapted yet. Take it nice and slow, letting your body adapt on its own time. Be mindful of which types of foods trigger cravings or cause you to overeat: for some people, it's cheese, and for others, it's other types of dairy, nuts, and seeds. Be careful with peanut butter and nut butters, such as cashew and almond butter; they can be a trigger for some people.

Aim to get 60 to 80 percent of your total calories from fat each day. Eat plenty of green vegetables, such as spinach, green cabbage, broccoli, cauliflower, and even algae, which are rich in potassium, an important micronutrient for optimal health. Use avocados, olives, avocado oil, and coconut oil in your cooking, and don't forget about mushrooms!

Ketosis tends to drain water and salt from your system, so drink water with a pinch of sea salt. Every gram of carbohydrate stores about a gram of water, which means that when eating keto, you won't store as much water as you used to.

TRUE AND FALSE KETOSIS

If you have been eating a low-carb, high-fat diet for some time and you have managed to shed your long-conditioned fear of fat, you might have no trouble at all reaching ketosis. But you might be one of those people who have detectable ketones in their blood, urine, and breath and still have a lot of extra weight to lose. Let me reveal the problem: your adrenal glands are out of whack, your body is under stress, and you aren't getting enough restorative sleep. As long as you have these types of imbalances, it will be very difficult for you to lose weight.

Treatable medical conditions are another reason why some people have trouble losing weight. Consult with your doctor and ask for a thyroid blood test if you suspect any underlying medical issues.

Another problem is that your meals might be too large and have too much extra fat added to them. If you eat meals like this, your body won't have the chance to use body fat for fuel because it will be burning dietary fat instead. Even if your metabolic rate is a bit higher in ketosis, there's still an energy limit at which your body is content with using the fat it's being fed and not the fat around your waist. I call this "false" ketosis because you are not really a fat-burner if you are burning dietary fat rather than stored fat.

If you feel that this description applies to you, don't fast. Eat breakfast, lunch, and dinner. Go to bed between 9:30 and 10:30 p.m. Sleep for at least seven hours and stay away from unnatural blue light (from computers, smartphones, tablets, and TV screens) for several hours before bedtime. If avoiding screens at night is impossible for you, buy yellow, orange, or red protective glasses and wear them from 7:00 p.m. until bedtime. They will help you get your sleep hormone, melatonin, on time and give you better sleep in general. Plenty of blue-light-blocking apps are available for computers and phones—I recommend them if you spend a lot of time in front of your computer at night, like I do.

Do everything you can to reduce stress. Try yoga, meditation, or other mindfulness exercises. Be mindful of your body, your breathing, and your thoughts and feelings. Try to identify what kinds of thoughts or feelings you have prior to a food craving, for example, and remember that what seems like hunger is sometimes really thirst. Drink a lot of water—several quarts a day—and don't forget to add some salt to it.

YOUR IDEAL WEIGHT

The ketogenic diet will optimize your hormones, which will lead you to reach your optimal weight. It might be higher than you want it to be, or it might be just perfect—but it won't be static. Your ideal weight will depend on your age, gender, muscle mass, and current weight.

In 1953, British physician Gordon Kennedy presented a hypothesis about how mammals regulate their body weight according to a reference point that relates to energy intake and amount of body fat. It means that two people with totally different weights can eat the same amount, and both will maintain their individual weight. It also means that long-term calorie restriction will acclimate the body to a very low calorie intake and relate that intake to a certain amount of body fat. That is why many overweight people can't lose weight on low-calorie diets, which is one reason a high-fat diet is superior. With a high-fat diet, your body won't lower its metabolic rate. Instead, it will increase its metabolic rate, as it has plenty of energy and doesn't need to conserve it.

The body strives for homeostasis, which is why it's important to maintain a new and lower body weight for as long as possible. Your current weight is your current set point, and if you gain or lose a few pounds, your body will want to go back to its set point. To change that set point to a more desirable weight, you need to maintain the new weight for at least six months. This is why you must be consistent with the ketogenic diet and not deviate from it one bit if you want to be done with yo-yo dieting.

Between 1 and 2 pounds (0.5 and 1 kg) of weight loss per week is optimal. If you try to lose weight faster than that, the risk of backfiring is greater. Try to keep calm and focus on feeling good rather than rushing the process.

BODY WEIGHT AND FAT PERCENTAGE

Low body weight does not equal a low body fat percentage. If you want to look fit, you will need to lower your body fat. Cellulite stems from fat and nothing else, so to get rid of cellulite, you need to increase your fat metabolism.

Before I started my keto diet, I had about 25 percent body fat. Today I have less than 15 percent body fat, even though my weight is higher, and I'm much more satisfied with the way my body looks. When

I was a tired, dispirited vegetarian, I always wanted to lose a few pounds to look more fit. I never feel that way now! I know that it's not about weight at all, and that body fat can easily be controlled with a keto diet.

How your fat is distributed tells a lot about your hormones. If you are a woman and all your fat is located in your breasts, butt, hips, and thighs, that is perfectly normal—it's a result of estrogen and insulin fat storage. Fat located primarily on your belly and back is a sign of unbalanced sex hormones and means that your estrogen could be a little low. Men primarily store fat on their midsection because of testosterone and insulin. When women get this type of fat distribution, it's a sign of high cortisol levels.

Men with extra fat on their breasts, hips, and thighs usually suffer from low testosterone levels; the more fat you carry, the more estrogen your body will produce. Body fat is not passive; it's actually an endocrine organ that produces hormones such as estrogen, leptin, and dopamine, to name a few. That is why excess body fat is a hormone disruptor.

Unnatural additives, such as high-fructose corn syrup, monosodium glutamate (MSG), hydrolyzed wheat, and processed sugars, grains, and starch, lead to unnatural fat distribution. Extra fat under the chin or on the upper arms or back is highly unnatural and can be a result of a prolonged intake of processed foods. Excess soy products can also cause unnatural fat distribution because they contain large amounts of xenoestrogens, which are molecules that mimic estrogens in the body. Two glasses of soy milk a day can be enough to disrupt a woman's menstrual cycle.

Weight gain on a natural diet will result in only a few extra pounds on the breasts, hips, and thighs in women and a few extra pounds around the midsection in men. The types of extreme obesity that are becoming more and more common can only stem from highly processed and industrialized food products with a high refined sugar content. Not only do processed foods result in weight gain with an unflattering fat distribution, but they also lead to hormonal issues, such as infertility, low sex drive, reduced attention span, depression, and chronic fatigue syndrome. A natural diet free from processed foods will improve these conditions, and weight loss will follow.

ENERGY AND MACRONUTRIENTS

Most types of meat contain about 20 percent protein; eggs contain 10 percent protein; and cheese is about 25 percent protein. Other dairy foods have about 10 percent protein, except for milk and cream, which have about 5 percent. Meats, fish, poultry, eggs, butter, lard, and coconut oil, as well as most cheeses, are almost completely free of carbohydrates. Leafy greens are very low in carbohydrates, too. Vegetables that grow above ground are also a safe bet.

Calculating macros and ratio of food intake is a bit tricky in the beginning, but it gets easier with a little practice. Nowadays there are a lot of phone apps and software programs to help you.

The first thing to get the hang of is carbohydrates. Check labels to see if there is any hidden sugar in your food. Another thing to watch out for is the number of ingredients listed on the label. If there are more than ten ingredients, it's not a natural product and should not be consumed. Put it back on the shelf! A good general rule is to buy only products with five or fewer ingredients.

To check whether you are on the right track, you can record everything you eat for a short time and divide the number of calories from fat by the total number of calories consumed. This number should be higher than 0.6, ideally around 0.8. Then you are ketogenic! I don't recommend food logging in general because it's far more important to learn how to read your body's signals of hunger and satiation, but logging can certainly be helpful until this becomes second nature to you.

Now, let's move on to protein, protein supplements, and other supplements on the ketogenic diet. I know that many people are curious about protein intake and how to choose the right supplements for optimal health, so let's dive in!

CHAPTER 7

FITNESS AND TRAINING
on a Ketogenic Diet

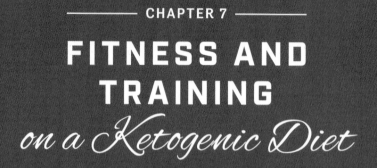

When you take advantage of your body's ability to use fat as fuel for the purpose of losing weight, you automatically get a better-looking body than you would with "normal" dieting. Calorie restriction causes you to lose both fat and muscle at the same time, while carb restriction eliminates only fat and water from your body. Eliminating fat and water gives you a tighter and more defined look without ever looking "skinny fat." As a bonus, you'll have plenty of energy throughout the day, and you'll never experience low blood sugar or energy depletion because your energy stores are more or less limitless when you refuel with fat rather than carbs.

When your body uses fat for fuel, you don't have to work out or do cardio to burn fat because you are already burning fat, regardless of whether you're watching TV, sleeping, or running. How cool is that?

WHY KETOSIS IS SUPERIOR FOR TRAINING

Ketones are small, water-soluble molecules that can serve as energy for both the brain and the muscles, which is why many people experience a range of benefits on a ketogenic diet. Increased endurance and faster muscle development are just two of them.

Endurance increases because less cellular lactate (i.e., lactic acid) accumulates in the muscles. The levels of both hydrogen and lactic acid increase due to high-intensity training, which generates a cascade of chemical reactions that eventually lead to fatigue. pH decreases because of the increasing amount of hydrogen ions. Another cause is the accumulation of blood lactate, the lactic acid in the blood that arises due to maximal oxygen consumption. Your individual threshold value for lactate then determines how much or for how long you can work out before you begin to feel the "burn" of lactic acid. With your increasing ability to use fat as an energy source, lactate production goes down and endurance goes up.

Your blood serum levels of oxygen and carbon dioxide control your breathing rate during intense exercise. When your brain registers low oxygen, your breathing rate increases. This causes an influx of oxygen, which increases carbon dioxide as a by-product. This carbon dioxide accumulates in the blood, leading to a decrease in pH, which also causes breathing to be heavier. Sometimes the accumulation of carbon dioxide even leads to hyperventilation.

A person who is keto-adapted accumulates less carbon dioxide and lactic acid, leading to a more stable blood pH. This gives a higher breathing quota of oxygen and carbon dioxide, which means that less carbon dioxide per calorie is consumed. Breathing quota refers to the amount of carbon dioxide that is needed for every oxygen molecule. When the body runs on glucose, that ratio is 1:1, thus the amounts of oxygen and carbon dioxide are the same. In ketosis, the ratio is generally about 0.7:1, which means that less carbon dioxide is needed. This explains the increase in energy distribution and oxygen absorption.

When my energy returned after I started my keto journey, running was the first kind of training I tried. At first, I could run only a couple hundred yards, but as I started to keto-adapt, I noticed an incredible difference in my endurance. Of course, the more I ran, the better I got at running. I also experienced a lot less build-up of lactic acid and began to feel as though I could run forever. I couldn't run any faster, but I could run for longer periods without getting tired—several hours, in fact.

KETOSIS AND MUSCLE GAINS

A fat cell is not 100 percent fat; it is 85 percent fat and 15 percent lean tissue. On a calorie-restricted diet, you generally lose both the fat and the lean tissue. However, in ketosis, fat-burning is much more specific. That means you will consume the portion of the fat cell that is pure fat, including some water, but not the 15 percent of the fat cell that is comprised of lean tissue. You literally gain muscle mass and lose body fat at the same time. For every kilogram (2.2 pounds) of fat that you lose, you automatically "gain" 150 grams (1¾ ounces) of lean tissue! This explains why body composition improves in ketosis.

BENEFITS OF TRAINING

Do you work out?

I didn't start exercising until after the age of 25, but it really is important to engage in some kind of physical activity. Most of us lead a sedentary lifestyle, which is unnatural considering that we are built for movement.

How you move really doesn't matter; what matters is that you actually do it. Set aside time for exercise at least a couple times a week.

Physical activity is not just about losing weight, and exercise shouldn't be used as an excuse to overeat. I believe that exercise is the best antidepressant available, and that we wouldn't need half of the drugs that doctors prescribe every day if we were more active, spent time outside running or hiking, went to the gym for some resistance training, or even just went out dancing.

Human beings are designed for natural movement that encompasses functional strength, durability, and explosiveness. The best training includes all three of these components, adjusted to your individual condition. In this chapter, I will focus on one of the most effective types of resistance training, called slow burn. However, any type of training that comprises all three basic concepts is good.

FUNCTIONAL STRENGTH

Two things are true about strength training: First, your muscles need to be activated throughout the whole exercise. Second, your muscles should be put under sufficient load to be able to grow in both volume and strength. This doesn't necessarily mean that you need to lift the maximum weight you can handle. The goal is to thoroughly activate your muscles. The basic principle of slow burn is to activate specific muscle groups by placing them under tension long enough for fast and efficient gains in strength.

Squats, lunges, and press-and-push exercises should be done slowly, with light weights or no weights at all. This is a hard concept for many gym rats to grasp, because they tend to think that heavier is better. That is not always the case, however. What really contributes to muscle growth is muscle activation and the length of time the muscles are under strain. Slow burn really works; there's a lot of science behind it. If you are already spending a lot of time in the gym and really like your own way of training, please try at least one slow-burn exercise just to feel the difference. The triceps push-down is a good exercise to do very slowly: do ten seconds of concentric (pushing) and ten seconds of eccentric. Do eight repetitions without stopping or pausing. You will definitely experience some pump and muscle activation.

If you are unfamiliar with the gym and gym exercises, don't worry; these exercises can be done both at home and in the gym, and you can use either barbells or a resistance band. The only rule is to do eight repetitions: ten seconds one way and ten seconds the other way—pushing or pulling. You need to do only one set per exercise. If this feels like too little, you can add more sets as you like. However, keep in mind that slow burn really is an efficient way to train.

Eight repetitions in one set means two minutes and forty seconds per muscle group, and that is two minutes and forty seconds of time under tension, which is a lot more than you would achieve during normal weight training. When weight training is done rapidly with heavy weights, there's even a risk that joints and ligaments might be affected more than the actual muscles. Such exercise doesn't build real strength; instead, it increases the risk of injuries. When you have successfully slow-burned a muscle group, you don't have to train that same muscle again for forty-eight to seventy-two hours. Just let it rest and grow, feeding it healthy fats and high-quality protein.

This is the smarter way of getting fit. Make sure that you really feel your muscles during the entire exercise and that the weight allows you to do eight repetitions, but not nine. When you can do more than eight repetitions, it's time to increase the weight. This is a scientifically proven method of activating both long and short muscle fibers. You can do all your gym exercises this way, whether they be push-ups, pull-ups, sit-ups, or free-weight training. This kind of exercise also increases core stability, balance, and coordination, which is especially important if you suffer from back pain. Slow burn exercise creates symmetry in the body so that discs and joints can cooperate without causing harm or pain.

Free weights are always better than gym machines because they include an element of balance and coordination. Standing up is better than sitting down. Ropes, barbells, and dumbbells are better than equipment that is fixed or forces you to work in a certain position. It's important to use movement patterns that are as natural as possible, both for functional training and to avoid injury.

ENDURANCE

Humans are designed for continuous movement and are born with amazing durability compared to all other animals. Running is second nature to us and therefore is a great way to exercise. Cycling, rowing, and swimming are great, too. However, if you are a beginner, just walking in nature can be a good start. If you have a pulse band or a smart watch that can detect your pulse, aim for 65 percent of your maximum pulse as a general guideline for training your heart and increasing endurance. To determine your maximum pulse, either you can do a max pulse test, which is strenuous, or you can calculate your max pulse from your age.

The usual equation is 220 − age = maximum heart rate (MHR). This does not always play out so well because many people can tolerate higher heart rates, while others can't attain the formula-driven number. This formula was empirically derived using young athletes. A 2001 study by Hirofumi Tanaka evaluated a broader age distribution and showed that this formula often underestimates max pulse in older subjects. A revised formula fitted to the data resulted in 208 − (0.7 * age) = MHR. If you are 68 years old, for example, the first formula gives you 220 − 68 = 152 MHR, while the second formula gives you 208 − (0.7 * 68) = 160.4 MHR.

HOW TO DETERMINE YOUR MHR

Do not try this without being darn sure that you're not going to drop dead. Before you do it, talk with your doctor. If you are worried about feeling uncomfortable during the test, don't try it.

Okay, with that warning out of the way, here's another method you can use to determine your MHR:

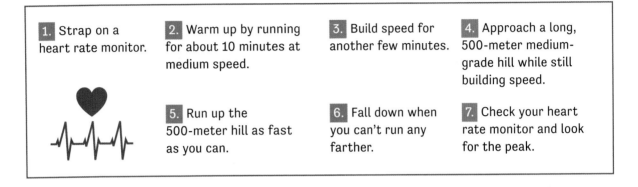

1. Strap on a heart rate monitor.

2. Warm up by running for about 10 minutes at medium speed.

3. Build speed for another few minutes.

4. Approach a long, 500-meter medium-grade hill while still building speed.

5. Run up the 500-meter hill as fast as you can.

6. Fall down when you can't run any farther.

7. Check your heart rate monitor and look for the peak.

If you're afraid of pushing yourself to your absolute max, just push yourself as far as you feel you can and then estimate the top end. Push yourself to what you think is 95 percent of your maximum and stop. Add 5 percent more beats per minute to your total. You'll very likely still be closer to your actual MHR than if you used the formula discussed on the previous page.

Even if you're not fit enough yet for endurance challenges, try to endure ten minutes of regular exercise a couple of times a week and gradually increase that time to thirty minutes. Pause during the exercise if it gets too exhausting. This type of exercise is great for increasing insulin sensitivity, increasing your flow of endorphins, and helping you keto-adapt more quickly.

Endorphins are a natural painkiller and antidepressant, so they have the power to improve your well-being on multiple levels.

EXPLOSIVITY

Explosivity is about working your heart and muscles hard during short bursts of intense movement. This exercise can be high-intensity interval training or weight lifting, which are very efficient in terms of weight loss and endurance. The idea is to reach 90 percent of your maximum heart rate for short periods, which releases testosterone and growth hormones to promote fat loss and well-being. It's also an efficient way to increase your durability—much faster than normal jogging.

THE HEALTH EFFECTS OF RESISTANCE TRAINING

The benefits of resistance training are threefold: metabolic, neuromuscular, and hormonal. The metabolic benefits are increased insulin sensitivity, a healthier heart, and an improved lipid profile. These effects are more clearly seen in endurance training but are not uncommon in resistance training. The neuromuscular benefits are healthier joints, muscles, and posture. Because most of us spend our days sitting, many of us suffer from aches and pains in the shoulders, back, and neck. Resistance training is a great way to alleviate these types of pain. The hormonal benefits are increased testosterone, growth hormones, and other growth factors that promote fat loss and muscle gains.

FREQUENCY

Movement is mandatory for optimal health; there's no way around it. If you don't work out, you should at least walk for twenty or thirty minutes a day—to start. Fill your smartphone with music or audio books and just do it. A totally sedentary lifestyle is very harmful.

Try to include some pulse training in your workout routine, whether it is running, walking, jogging, cycling, rowing, or swimming. Just a few minutes each week is a good start.

Resistance training can be done a couple of times a week for thirty to forty minutes each time. Make room in your schedule to invest in your health and well-being. Your future self will thank you!

SET GOALS

Work with your own set of conditions and set small, achievable goals. Don't set a goal to lose 20 pounds or to work out every day—keep it simple and fun to make continuous progress toward lasting change.

The most important thing is to keep your promises. If you plan to work out three times a week, make sure you do. If there's a single doubt in your mind that you will be able to manage two workouts a week, then start with just once a week. No goal is too small. When you have mastered one workout a week, increase it to two a week. This way you won't be overwhelmed, your self-esteem will increase, and your body will gradually adapt.

CHAPTER 8

PROTEIN
and
SUPPLEMENTS

Protein is a macronutrient that has always enjoyed a good reputation, regardless of the dietary source. However, because of its anti-ketogenic properties, protein should be somewhat limited on a ketogenic diet. You really don't need as much protein as you might think. Many people in the fitness world are addicted to protein and protein supplements. When I say "addicted," I mean literally addicted, because most protein supplements are based on milk proteins, which have addictive qualities. Another issue with protein is tolerance, which allows some athletes to eat several hundred grams of protein every day and claim that they need it. They don't! They have acclimated their bodies to a high and steady flow of protein, but the truth is that they would get much better results if they dared to try protein fasting once in a while.

You can try protein fasting on a ketogenic diet as well—it's really effective. Because a ketogenic diet moderates protein, you won't develop protein tolerance, meaning that you can experiment with different protein levels. This is particularly useful if you are into fitness or bodybuilding. I have found that a protein-free day every month or even every week can reset protein sensitivity and give muscle development a nice boost. To effectively protein fast, you need to have a fairly low body fat percentage and an interest in fitness; otherwise a protein fast is useless. Just keep your protein level below 40 percent of your daily intake and you will be fine with regard to weight loss and health improvements.

If you aren't into sports and don't work out intensely several days a week, there is no need for you to get extra protein in the form of protein powder or protein bars. Most of these products are highly processed and contain a lot of sugar alcohols, dietary fiber, and artificial sweeteners that trigger hunger, cravings, and overeating. This is especially true of protein bars and low-carb bars. Another negative aspect of these products is that they can cause bloating and water retention. If you are hungry for a snack, eat an avocado, a boiled egg, or some macadamia nuts instead.

ABOUT PROTEIN

Humans need protein to survive, but excess protein is unnecessary; it will only be converted to glucose and hinder both fat metabolism and ketone production. Protein contains a lot of nitrogen, which is a bit acidic to the body. Too much nitrogen can temporarily impede muscle development and even lower testosterone levels. Your body can process only about 20 grams of protein at a time.

Four eggs are enough to cover your immediate protein needs after a hard workout. If you are doing heavy weight training and insist on supplementing with whey protein, you will never need more than 30 grams a day. Also, remember that real foods are sufficient for proper muscle development. You should consider trying other types of protein powders, such as egg, beef, and collagen, which are far less inflammatory than whey protein.

If you are a vegetarian, a mix of 30 percent rice protein and 70 percent pea protein supplies a complete amino profile with a minimum of carbohydrates. Just because a food is high in protein doesn't mean that your body can use it, which is why protein profiles and bioavailability need to be considered.

There's a huge difference between types of protein, depending on the source, how they're broken down, and how the body uses them. For example, proteins from peanuts have very low bioavailability for humans. We can utilize only a few percent; the rest is converted to glucose. The better a protein's bioavailability, the more of it we can use and the less it affects our blood glucose levels. Animal proteins are the best match for us, so we don't need much of it to satisfy our needs.

Beans are generally high in protein, but they have a pretty low biocompatibility for humans. However, some beans, such as kidney beans, are a decent source of resistant starch. Resistant starch is a great supplement for the gut flora, especially on a keto diet, because it doesn't affect insulin levels. Resistant starch feeds the good bacteria in your gut, improving gut health and the immune system. It also lowers blood glucose levels, which is great for pre-diabetics and people with high blood glucose. If you work out and have good insulin sensitivity, you can try adding a cup of kidney beans to your diet each week.

Another keto-approved source of resistant starch is a tablespoon of potato flour dissolved in a glass of water; or you can eat a cold boiled potato. This is also a remedy for low serotonin and can have a positive influence on your mood if you often feel depressed.

HOW MUCH PROTEIN IS ENOUGH?

The amount of protein you need depends on your lifestyle. If you don't work out much and you want to lose weight, you will need only about 0.6 grams of protein per kilogram (2.2 pounds) of fat-free mass. Another general rule is that you should consume a number of grams of protein equal to your ideal weight. So if you want to weigh 132 pounds (60 kilograms), you should eat 60 grams (about 2 ounces) of protein per day.

The more you work out, the more protein you need—but not more than 1.5 grams of protein per kilogram (2.2 pounds) of fat-free mass. A common guideline is that if you do heavy workouts, such as weight lifting or CrossFit, you need less than 100 grams (3½ ounces) of protein per day if you're a woman or less than 200 grams (7 ounces) per day if you're a man.

A consistent intake of protein from high-quality sources coupled with a high ratio of healthy fats promotes weight loss, muscle development, efficient fat metabolism, and ketone production.

AMINO ACIDS

Amino acids are biologically important organic compounds that comprise the second-largest component of human muscles, cells, and other tissues. (The largest component is water.) Amino acids are the constituent parts of all protein and perform critical roles in such processes as neurotransmitter transport and biosynthesis. Eating protein from natural sources with high biocompatibility is vitally important because it is critical to these functions. People who consistently choose poor protein sources, such as processed meats, soy, or legumes, often have weak hair and nail growth, wrinkles, and poor muscle development.

If you want an efficient protein supplement for your workouts, I suggest amino acids rather than whey or casein protein. Amino acids are much more effective and potent, and you need a lot less of them.

There are a lot of amino acids to choose from, and many of them are wonderful supplements! Most amino acids are glucogenic, which means that they are converted to glucose through gluconeogenesis. This is in contrast to the ketogenic amino acids, which are converted to ketone bodies.

One beneficial glucogenic amino acid is L-glutamine, which is a great help when you have severe cravings. It relieves sugar cravings effectively. Another is L-glycine, which has the capacity to lower cortisol levels and improve sleep. Take a teaspoon of L-glycine in a cup of hot water before bed and see if it works for you. Some people experience adverse but rare effects such as heart palpitations.

The nine essential amino acids—phenylalanine, valine, threonine, tryptophan (a precursor to serotonin!), leucine, isoleucine, lysine, and histidine—are both glucogenic and ketogenic. However, humans can't synthesize them, so they must be gotten via diet and/or supplements. All nine of these amino acids can be taken in a supplement called essential amino acids, or EAA. EAA contains the most important amino acids from whey protein in pre-metabolized form, which means that you need a lot less of it. Among the essential amino acids, lysine is the only one that is purely ketogenic.

If you want to be even more specific and target only the most muscle-building amino acids, you can try BCAA instead. BCAA contains the branched-chain amino acids leucin, isoleucine, and valine. Leucin is the only purely ketogenic branched-chain amino acid. Isoleucine is both ketogenic and glucogenic, and valine is purely glucogenic.

Leucin is the amino acid that affects muscle growth the most significantly, and it is ketogenic. However, for maximum muscle response, leucin is more effective if taken with the other BCAAs. You need only about 5 grams of BCAA per day, as it has the same effect as 20 grams of whey protein.

If you're not interested in fitness and bodybuilding, you don't need any extra protein, either BCAA or EAA.

Amino acids play many different roles in the body, and by adding them to your diet, you can boost any area you like. L-arginine, for example, increases sex drive, while L-citrulline increases endurance and oxygen availability during high-intensity training. L-tyrosine can increase your metabolism if combined with iodine salt because tyrosine and iodine are the building blocks of important thyroid hormones.

As you can see, there are many interesting things to learn about amino acids. I could probably write an entire book about them; the same goes for other supplements, as well as vitamins and minerals.

OTHER SUPPLEMENTS ON A KETO DIET

Before I started the keto diet, I gave vitamins a try to see if they would improve my energy levels and general health, but I didn't notice a difference. I find that many people take vitamins just because they think they should, because vitamins are supposed to be good for them. My philosophy is that if you don't notice any improvement from a supplement, you should stop taking it!

The reason people seldom get revolutionary effects from vitamins is that the recommended dose for most vitamins is about one-tenth of the effective dose. If you follow the instructions on the bottle, the amount you take will likely be too little to produce a noticeable effect. Vitamin C is a great example of a vitamin that comes in mini-doses. The effective dose of vitamin C is more than 1 gram a day, and preferably 3 to 5 grams a day in the form of pure crystallized powder. The same goes for vitamin D, magnesium, selenium, and CoQ10, which are other great supplements when taken in the right amounts. I encourage you to search the internet for effective therapeutic doses and learn more about each supplement.

Never buy multivitamins. It's important to take each vitamin singly, in the right form and for the right purpose. Some vitamins should be crystallized powder, and others need to be in liquid form. Never buy vitamins that have sugar added to them, either. Supplements that look and taste like candy *are* candy!

Magnesium, sodium, and potassium are needed for a normal electrolyte balance, especially on a keto diet. There are about twelve different types of magnesium with completely different effects; do your homework before you buy. Magnesium oxide relieves constipation and leg cramps. Magnesium malate increases energy levels. Magnesium citrate is good for anxiety. Magtein improves memory. Most types of magnesium lower heart rate and blood pressure as well. You don't need extra potassium if you eat leafy greens and avocado.

If you are worried about acidity on a keto diet, you can add a sulfur supplement such as MSM (methylsulfonylmethane), which is an alkaline supplement that promotes gut health and the health of skin, hair, and nails. Zinc is also beneficial for the connective tissues and can be a helpful aid if you suffer from estrogen dominance as well as increased cortisol levels. Zinc picolinate is the form of zinc with the highest bioavailability.

A complete diet that is rich in nutrient-dense foods eliminates the need for most supplements, so fixing your diet is the number-one priority before you decide to add any.

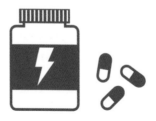

CHAPTER 9

CARBOHYDRATES

I've discussed protein, fats, and even exercise and how they relate to the ketogenic diet. Now it's time to talk a little about carbohydrates. This chapter is fairly short because there's no reason to talk at length about carbohydrates when you're on a keto diet. There's a small amount of carbohydrate in most foods, such as vegetables, nuts, and berries, but they don't pose a problem as long as you're eating healthful natural foods.

Carbohydrates are not evil in essence. Glucose is an important molecule for all forms of life on earth. However, we want to exclude most carbs because they exist in such excess in our modern world. The number-one goal on a ketogenic diet is to eat foods that are as natural and unprocessed as possible and inevitably to end up with a limited carb intake.

Choosing foods solely based on their carbohydrate content won't do the trick, because many low-carb foods and drinks are not healthy at all. Sugar-free sodas, low-carb bars, and other commercial food items labeled "low-carb" are often bad choices. Whiskey, vodka, and rum have close to zero carb content but are not particularly good for you. The same thinking should apply to everything.

Look at the labels and study the food products. Ask yourself if the product you're considering is a natural and healthy for your body. If not, pass on it. Can you pronounce the names of the ingredients? Do most of the ingredients seem to consist of letters and numbers? If the answer is yes, then that food is probably not a good choice.

Never choose a processed food over a natural one just because the processed food has fewer carbs.

CARBS AND FITNESS

There's a huge misunderstanding about the role of carbohydrates in training and muscle development. Many people who choose a low-carb diet to lose weight eventually choose to go back to a high-carb diet to reach their fitness goals. This is totally unnecessary. Carbs are not building blocks in the synthesis of muscle protein—amino acids are. When you are in ketosis, you will gain lean muscle mass while losing body fat, just as you will gain lean muscle mass at the gym when you perform resistance training. This gain in muscle mass comes from proteins in foods being broken down into amino acids and triggering the metabolic processes of muscle development.

It might seem as though a carb-eater is gaining more muscle mass when training, but that's because every gram of carbohydrate binds about 4 grams of water. On the contrary, a ketogenic diet drains water and eliminates bloating, giving you a more defined look. No extra "fluff" is being added.

Muscles, in combination with water and fat, can create an illusion of volume, but once you are keto-adapted, your muscles will look nice and full without carbs. Carbohydrates are 100 percent anti-ketogenic because they raise both blood glucose and insulin levels. Also, because insulin is a storage hormone, it can aid the body in transporting amino acids and nutrients to the muscles. It's also quickly and easily absorbed energy, so it does play a role in fitness. The increase in insulin might also activate other growth factors, giving muscle development a little boost. However, carbohydrates are not needed to boost muscle development. Ketosis is a metabolic state that allows optimal hormonal responses without the need for insulin. The most muscle-producing amino acid—the ketogenic L-leucine— can be active in the bloodstream for several hours while in ketosis, continuing to signal growth to muscle cells during that time.

Another advantage of the keto diet is that you won't need to go on a diet after gaining muscle because you will already be lean. You can work out for longer periods; you don't need to time your meals or bring protein shakes to the gym; and you won't hit the wall. When your blood sugar is flat-lining throughout the day, it doesn't matter whether you ate eight hours ago or two hours ago. Your body will have an optimal flow of fuel regardless of your food intake and will continue to feed your muscles energy even after the workout. Take the time to keto-adapt and experience the enormous benefits of gaining strength and muscle while in ketosis, regardless of your fitness level.

Most fitness experts will disagree with what I'm saying here. Then again, they are not keto-adapted, nor do they understand the intricacies of human metabolism. The more you read about this subject, the more you will understand. I wrote this book to inspire and motivate you. Don't blindly believe what I am telling you; rather, try it out for yourself and see if it holds true for you.

Remember that you build muscles by training them, not specifically by food intake. Another important thing to keep in mind is that it's not possible to convert fat to muscle; there is no such biochemical process. Fat is fat and cannot become anything other than fat. That means you shed fat by changing your food choices, not by exercising.

KETOSIS = ENDLESS ENERGY

Your glycogen stores hold about 2,000 calories compared to an average body fat storage of more than 40,000 calories. Even a very lean person will have many, many times more energy in the form of fat than glycogen. Because ketones can fuel both explosive and slow muscle fibers, there's no doubt about which metabolic state is more beneficial. The more you use ketones and fat, the better your capacity will be to use fat as a fuel, which in turn saves a lot of glycogen. The result is that you will always have a glycogen store ready for high-intensity bursts if you need it.

If you don't want to keto-adapt but do want to lower your carbs to achieve a leaner look, you can add complex carbs before workouts or a couple of times a week or month based on your body and fitness level. Many athletes use refeeds, in which they eat one meal with a high carb content each week or month to replenish their glycogen stores. Especially popular among bodybuilders, this approach is known as a cyclic ketogenic diet. The ketogenic days allow the body to shed water and fat, and the refeeds add to visual muscle volume. It's a technique that has been proven to work for many athletes, even if they never keto-adapt and never use the full potential of ketosis. I don't personally believe in refeeds because keto-adaptation is better in the long run, but some people find success with this method. However, I do not recommend refeeding if you have a lot of weight to lose because it will only interfere with weight loss.

Men generally have a higher tolerance for carbohydrates than women because estrogen influences insulin sensitivity. This is probably why most of the people on cyclic ketogenic diets are men with a low body fat percentage.

KETONES FOR CLARITY

The most important impact of ketones on my daily life is improved mental clarity. I need to think clearly in order to write, invent, and create, and keto benefits me greatly. Constant fluctuations in blood sugar make it difficult to keep your attention on one thing at a time. Scientific studies have shown that intelligence and memory worsen with a high sugar intake, which correlates to my own experience in studying that type of food.

KETONES LOWER INFLAMMATION

Refined sugar is highly inflammatory and is the cause of many modern lifestyle diseases, including cancer. A cancer cell has ten times more insulin receptors on its surface than a healthy human cell and uses up to 200 times more glucose. This means that higher blood glucose levels promote the growth of potential cancer cells.

Eating real food lowers the risk of a wide variety of diseases and is a great way to manage blood sugar, insulin, and inflammatory markers. Whole foods also enable you to work out more intensely and for longer periods because they improve your body's repair mechanisms.

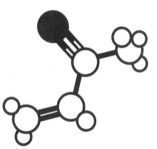

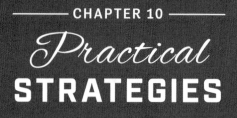

CHAPTER 10

Practical
STRATEGIES

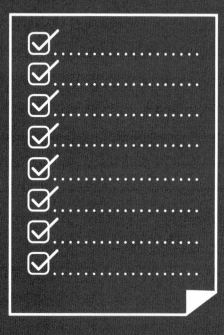

As I've mentioned before, the ketogenic diet is not a quick fix—it's a lifestyle. Transitioning into ketosis can be quite challenging for many people because it is a completely new way of thinking and relating to food. This chapter offers some tips and tricks to help you handle any obstacles that might arise.

The first and most important tip is not to focus on your weight for a while. Please don't weigh yourself daily. Women's weight in particular tends to fluctuate wildly because of hormonal cycles, water retention, and other phenomena. This is normal. If water retention bothers you, buy some nettle or dandelion tea at the supermarket or a health food store—it's a natural diuretic. Remember, weight loss is never linear. Even if you gain several pounds from one day to the next, it is not fat, only water and stomach contents.

Another thing to consider is hormonal health and your current hormonal status. A ketogenic diet will get you on the right track, but there are a lot of useful medicines as well. A test of your levels of cortisol and sex hormones (testosterone, estrogen, and progesterone) could reveal a lot about your current health status. Also, you can learn a great deal by testing your fasting blood glucose and long-term blood glucose levels. Invest in a glucometer and urine test strips for ketones.

First, let's review the most common mistakes to make sure you don't fall into any of these categories:

1. YOU'RE EATING TOO MANY CARBS. Check labels and learn about the carb contents of different types of food. Don't be afraid to eliminate all carbs from your diet just to see what it feels like and to make sure you transition into full-blown ketosis. Remember that you really don't need carbohydrates to thrive, so you can experiment with your individual threshold.

I'm quite active, so I can handle about 50 grams of carbohydrates a day, but I prefer to keep it between 5 and 20 grams a day, and I have been doing so for several years. I discussed carbohydrates in Chapter 9, and by now you know that you can use them sparingly in an effort to improve your fitness level. If your main objective is to lose weight, you'll want to keep carbs as low as possible. Also, make sure you don't eat "sugar-free" products, because they might influence your blood sugar. If your blood sugar is too high, you won't lose any weight, so you need to handle this issue first.

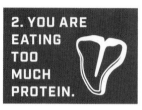

2. YOU ARE EATING TOO MUCH PROTEIN. As you know, proteins are more glucogenic than ketogenic, so if you usually eat a lot of dry, fat-free chicken or whitefish, you might consider trying fattier types of meat and fish, such as salmon and pork. Just changing the types of animal protein you eat can make a big difference. Don't be afraid to use butter, lard, or other types of healthy fat in your cooking.

The list on pages 290 and 291 outlines appropriate ketogenic food choices. As discussed in Chapter 8, most protein supplements are unnecessary. Don't be deceived by the low calorie content, because it's not about calories—it's about hormone response.

3. YOU'RE AFRAID OF EATING FAT. That leads me to my next point: fear of fat. That fear is just not compatible with a ketogenic diet. You need to lose your fear. I know it's hard. We have been brainwashed into believing that fat will make us fat. But in fact, fat and cholesterol are essential for optimal weight and health! Chapters 5 and 6 explore fat and cholesterol in some detail. Please reread them if you are in doubt.

4. YOU ARE NOT REPLENISHING SODIUM.

When your insulin levels drop on a ketogenic diet, your body will shed excess water and sodium along with it. This is why people get rid of excess bloat after a few days of low-carb eating.

Sodium, however, is a crucial electrolyte in the body. A lack of sodium is one of the main reasons people experience side effects on the ketogenic diet, such as light-headedness, fatigue, headaches, and even constipation. To solve the problem, simply add a pinch of salt to every meal!

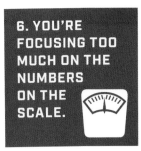

6. YOU'RE FOCUSING TOO MUCH ON THE NUMBERS ON THE SCALE.

Chapters 7 and 8, which deal with body fat, fat metabolism, and training, touch on the fact that your body composition will change on a keto diet. Those changes might mean that you don't lose any actual weight, just body fat. Some people lose weight that you can see. Others don't lose any weight at all, but look better and experience greatly improved health. Weight loss isn't the most important thing.

Your chances of not losing weight increase if you are already lean or have a low body weight. I actually *gained* several pounds after being on the keto diet for a while, though my body composition improved.

5. YOU AREN'T BEING PATIENT.

When I was coaching people, I had clients who expected to see results within two or three days, and that was just not going to happen. It's normal to feel like something the cat dragged in during the first few days on a keto diet. However, you need to stick with it and let your body heal from within. A few weeks of low-carb eating is nothing in the long run. If you are serious about optimizing your health and being the best possible version of yourself, you need to give it time. It's a process, and you will be better—and continue to improve—for as long as you live.

Your body is designed to burn carbs for as long as they are available. Because carbs have been available in excess your entire life, your body is not used to using fat for energy. If you are sensitive, you might even experience low-carb flu. I certainly did, because I was very carb-dependent. Low-carb flu makes you feel sick, tired, and low on energy for a few days, but it will pass. It's most often caused by a lack of energy from food. If you drastically decrease your carb intake and have a fear of fat at the same time, you will end up with no carbs and no energy. As you might expect, the experience will not be pleasant. Drink water, add salt to your meals, and eat more food. Have an avocado and some black olives. Eat some leafy greens and go for a walk; you will feel a lot better.

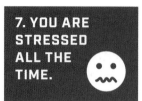

7. YOU ARE STRESSED ALL THE TIME.

Your body and mind are connected; you are what you think. If you are stressed out about your weight, your health, or your job situation, it will be difficult for you to keto-adapt and lose weight. Stress increases cortisol and inhibits weight loss. Make sure that you sleep enough, and work on the mental aspects of your life—it's really important.

8. YOU'RE NOT EATING REAL FOOD.

The ketogenic diet is not just about lowering your carb intake. It's mostly about eating real food from trustworthy sources. Skip the treats, even if they are made with healthy ingredients, and eliminate all sweeteners!

9. YOU'RE EATING TOO MANY NUTS AND DAIRY PRODUCTS.

Leave them out if you get stuck or if you are having trouble getting into ketosis. You don't need nuts, seeds, or dairy in your diet at all, so the less of them you eat, the better.

10. YOU DON'T EXERCISE.

Don't exercise with the goal of burning calories. Again, it's not about calories; it's about your hormones. Exercise is great for lowering blood glucose and cortisol levels and increasing general happiness. Exercise is also about improving your metabolic health, so start exercising and focus on the joy of movement.

REASONS YOU MAY BE HAVING TROUBLES KETO-ADAPTING

- Vitamin D deficiencies
- Trace mineral deficiencies
- Poor gut flora
- Adrenal stress
- Elevated cortisol
- Poor sleep
- Caffeine
- Cheese
- Nuts
- Low stomach acid
- Overtraining
- Too much protein
- Clogged liver
- Autoimmune disorder
- Allergies
- Poor thyroid health
- Not enough fat
- Leaky gut
- Inflammation
- Low sex hormone
- Stress

Every one of these conditions deserves a book of its own. It is super-important to heal your body, mind, and gut first because any imbalances will interfere with your other goals. Stress is a major issue today, and it affects us in more ways than we could ever imagine. Stress affects our hormones, our weight, our thoughts, and our entire lives. I'm not going to tell you to commit to a stress-free life (but I really want to). Physical exercise, yoga, meditation, and even walks in nature are great stress relievers.

Lack of vitamin D and important trace elements can make it harder to keto-adapt. Experiment with magnesium, sodium, zinc, and potassium supplements to see if they improve your mental and physical well-being. Eat at least 50 grams of spinach every day to replenish your potassium levels. Remember that avocados are rich in potassium as well.

Poor gut flora is another reason people have difficulties keto-adapting. Consume resistant starch to improve your gut health, and try high-quality probiotics from a reputable health food store. To be effective, probiotics need to contain at least 10 billion bacteria from ten different strains and preferably not be derived from milk products (to avoid inflammation). Only buy probiotics that list all the strains on the bottle. Don't buy probiotics from supermarkets because those products likely contain a lot of added sugar. Milk and dairy foods are not good sources of probiotics. Instead, add some pickled vegetables or apple cider vinegar to your diet. As mentioned previously, potato starch and kidney beans can be great options, too.

High blood sugar can be battled with exercise, long walks, fasting, and the supplements Gymnema Sylvestre, Ceylon cinnamon, and chromium. Drink warm lemon water to aid digestion, because constipation is quite common during the first two weeks on a keto diet.

Warm lemon water can also help the liver with detoxing, as can cruciferous vegetables, dandelion, ginger, and the supplement milk thistle.

If you have a lot of cravings due to unregulated blood sugar, try peppermint oil or peppermint tea. Both are great for curbing cravings.

STRATEGIES FOR WEIGHT PLATEAUS

Because weight loss isn't linear, it's completely normal to experience weight plateaus. If it's a stubborn one, try eating different types of food than you normally eat. If you usually eat a lot of red meat, for example, switch to seafood. If you eat a lot of nuts and/or berries, omit them completely for a couple of weeks and see what happens. Also change up the varieties of vegetables you are eating.

Don't be afraid to experiment to see how your body reacts to certain types of foods or to experience real hunger. You can do so by fasting once a week or trying intermittent fasting, where you restrict your eating to a certain window of time each day. Be careful with fasting; if you have a food addiction or severe adrenal problems, it may only worsen the situation. In these cases, breakfast is the most important meal in order to avoid reversed cortisol and to eliminate hunger and cravings throughout the day. Reversed cortisol implies low morning cortisol, making you tired and sleepy in the morning no matter how many cups of coffee you drink. It also implies high evening cortisol, which means that you're not tired when you should to be. Instead of sleeping, you might be in bed late at night scrolling through social media on your smartphone or restlessly tossing and turning.

You can also try varying the size of your meals, making them smaller or larger. Experiment with more or less green vegetables, meat, fish, and fats.

If you are curious about intermittent fasting, there are several types you can try. The most popular is 16:8, which means that you fast for sixteen hours and then have an eight-hour eating window. Fasting generally works better for men than for women. Men experience more benefits and less hunger during a fast. If you want to do a twenty-four-hour (or longer) fast, you can have a hard-boiled egg or an avocado when your hunger is too strong. Eat a full meal after the fast.

The metabolic benefits of fasting are that it resets your system, lowers insulin, lowers blood glucose, and increases growth hormone and other fat-burning hormones. Fasting will also give you a more accurate understanding of what real hunger feels like. Real hunger is a subtle feeling indicating that your energy levels need to be replenished. Also, you will likely feel like eating "real food" rather than junk. Hunger triggered by blood sugar irregularities is not real. Acute and panicked feelings of hunger are more psychological or emotional types of hunger than actual physiological ones.

Fasting is completely safe unless you suffer from a severe illness. Some types of medication are not compatible with fasting, so if you are unsure, consult your doctor first. As long as you're relatively healthy and not diabetic, you don't need to worry that your energy levels or blood sugar will hit rock-bottom and kill you. The world record for fasting is held by a man who fasted for 382 straight days in the 1960s. No food at all—only water, vitamins, and minerals. It took place in England and involved an extremely obese man who had two choices: lose weight fast or die. Doctors monitored his health closely throughout the whole period. After the fast was over, the man had reached a perfectly normal weight of 176 pounds (80 kilograms). I am not suggesting that everybody should consider such extreme measures, but I assure you that *anyone* should be able to endure a few hours without food!

Remember that fasting means no food at all—only water and perhaps some tea or coffee. Anything you eat will break the fast, unless you are fasting for more than twenty-four hours (in which case you can eat a hard-boiled egg or an avocado if you get too hungry). When you start eating again after a fast, start with fat because it will be the most satiating and will also impede any adverse insulin response from protein and carbohydrates (fat positively affects the rate at which the other macronutrients hit your bloodstream).

Before you close this book and embark on your journey toward optimal health, let me share some final thoughts with you.

What most people don't realize is that making a big lifestyle change in terms of fitness and health is a significant psychological challenge. When making a big lifestyle change such as adopting a ketogenic diet, your thoughts and attitude are what matter, not how many pounds you still have to lose to reach your goal weight. How you feel on a day-to-day basis is what determines your chance of success. You need to realize the value of being your own best friend rather than your own worst enemy. You need to be your own greatest supporter and companion and take full responsibility for your health; after all, no one else is going to do it for you! Your family can't do it for you, nor can your doctors, the healthcare system, or society.

Many people treat their bodies like rental cars that they can crash and swap for a new one. You have only one body, and it needs your attention every single day. Cater to its every need and take appropriate measures when it's not working properly. A great meditation is to "feel" your body from within, turning your attention inward as often as you can and shifting your focus from body to mind.

While committing to be the best version of yourself that you can possibly be, it's important to remember that it's worth a great deal—certainly more than the slight discomfort of turning down unhealthy food alternatives when you're out with friends or saying no to things that make you feel stressed out. It's not about any other person—it's about you. The most important thing is to feel good, and you can't feel good if you are inflamed, tired, or stressed or you eat or drink excessively. You deserve to be in control, to be healthy, vibrant, and happy. This is not something you can put off to some vague future date. Get started right now—not tomorrow or next week, but today!

Set inspiring goals for this quest, write down a plan for the week, and have a look at the recipes in this book, beginning on page 124. Check out the meal plan in the following chapter and the food list on pages 290 and 291. Arrange a walk or workout with a friend and commit to it. You won't regret it.

Six months from now, you will thank yourself. You will say, "Yes, it was hard in the beginning, but I'm so grateful that I took the leap and really made a lasting change. I'm thankful that I didn't give up, that I dedicated myself fully and completely. I am thankful that I reached a whole new level of fitness and health that I didn't think existed."

I promise you that if you just keep at it, there is no limit to the things you can accomplish. All you need are consistency and focus. Don't focus on what you don't want, on what you don't like, or on the obstacles. Focus on the new you— how you want to feel and what type of body you want. Think about the types of clothes you will be able to wear and the new energy you will experience when your body doesn't have to deal with all that junk anymore.

Focus and consistency go hand in hand. When you deviate, you lose your focus, and when you lose your focus, you deviate. Keep your eyes on the prize!

Be careful with alcohol, substitute products, and carbohydrates until your body has become keto-adapted. Stay consistent, and take it one day at a time. You don't need to make a lifelong commitment never to eat a doughnut or an ice cream cone again. You can eat whatever you want, but *not right now.* You can have that piece of chocolate cake, but *not right now.* Make the healthier choices and let your body thrive. You will watch with wonder how your body composition improves, your skin improves, your hair and nails improve, and your sleep and vitality improve.

Everything you do matters because *you* matter. Your thoughts, feelings, and actions have a great effect on you, as well as on your surroundings. That's why it's so important to have a loving and honest relationship with yourself. If you spoke to your best friend the way you talk to yourself, would that person still be your best friend?

Honesty is also important when something doesn't work for you, because if you're not acknowledging it, you can't fix it. Always look at the facts when it comes to body, mind, food, and health. If you're not feeling all right, acknowledge it. If you're overweight, acknowledge it. If you don't exercise enough, you overeat, or you cheat—acknowledge it. If something doesn't work for you, try something else, and if that doesn't work, try something else again. Keep trying different approaches until you get the results you want—that's the fastest road to success in any area.

As you can see, the ketogenic diet is a lot more than a diet. It's a lifestyle and a way to get to know yourself and your body intimately. Use your physical and psychological feelings and sensations as a road map. If you don't usually tune in to them, now is the time to start. A lot of people live in the emotional dark ages and pay no attention to their emotions until they have, say, a heart attack. Don't let this happen to you! You have an emotional signaling system for a reason, and it can help you every step of the way.

Not paying attention to your feelings is like driving your car with no map, no GPS, and no headlights in the dark. You know better. You have learned a lot about hormones and human biochemistry by reading this book! Now you are well equipped for success. Regardless of how you choose to use this information, it is yours, whether you want to lose weight, get fit, improve your health, or just feel good.

I wish you the best of luck!

Martina Johansson
Shanghai, 2017

30-Day
MEAL PLAN

This section lays out a thirty-day meal plan for a standardized ketogenic diet. The plan will put you in ketosis and is best accompanied by light training. Even if you are already quite fit and used to heavy workouts, lighter training is necessary during the transition period. Avoid high-intensity workouts, running, and weight lifting; stick to walking and light resistance training instead.

The transition can take weeks or even months, as it is a process of healing. Don't rush it. If you have adrenal fatigue, chronic inflammation, high blood pressure, elevated blood sugar, or other imbalances that need to heal before major weight loss can occur, you need to focus on your general health and not on the number on the scale. Whether you are overweight, underweight, or at your ideal weight, the most important thing is to feel good. We all have different ideals and goals, but if we don't prioritize our mental and physical health, it will be very difficult to reach them.

It is tempting to believe that once you have reached a certain weight or body shape, everything else will magically fall into place. The truth is, no matter what your goal, you have to work hard from the start. It's not going to be easy. You will have to demand more of yourself than ever before. Most people have some form of substance addiction, whether it is nicotine, caffeine, sugar, gluten, or dairy proteins, and it is a challenge to break habits that are hard-wired into your brain—especially if you are biochemically inclined to develop chemical addictions. Therefore, the goal of this thirty-day plan is to make the keto diet work for you, not to scare you away. The keto diet is not an easy thing to master. Rather than give up, make adjustments as you see fit and move along at your own pace.

A clean diet should be free from the addictive substances I just mentioned, but being a coffee drinker myself, I cannot demand that you quit just like that. I quit caffeine a few times and know that for me, it's beneficial for both weight loss and my energy level. Many diet pills contain caffeine or variations of the caffeine molecule, but taking them is counterproductive, as they affect blood sugar negatively. You probably know by now that anything that messes with your blood sugar also messes with your moods, energy level, and hunger signals.

That said, try to limit your caffeine intake, but you don't need to avoid it entirely. Many people love butter coffee (see my Fatty Coffee recipe on page 238) and find it beneficial to drink while fat fasting and employing other tricks to get into ketosis more quickly. Coffee and tea are generally better alternatives than caffeinated drinks because they contain fewer chemical additives.

Dairy products are in the gray zone. Even though they are quite addictive and can inhibit weight loss, some full-fat dairy shouldn't cause you too much trouble. I use a little hard cheese and heavy cream here and there, and it's fine as long as I don't make it a daily habit.

Nuts and seeds are always dubious food choices. Just like dairy, they shouldn't be consumed every day. When you do eat them, make sure to soak or roast them first. Doing so eliminates most of their anti-nutrients.

Sweeteners are another subject of debate in the keto community. I personally use stevia or powdered sugar substitutes when I make desserts, but consuming sweeteners every day would seriously affect your gut flora, as well as your taste buds! Get rid of all "sugar-free" products, including chewing gums and cough syrups.

HOW TO HANDLE CRAVINGS

Sugar and gluten are big no-nos, of course! If you suddenly crave these substances, you may have fallen into the common trap of eating too few calories. It happens to most people on the keto diet because of reduced feelings of hunger. When you are in ketosis, you will not crave food the same way, so hunger signals are easy to miss. Don't be afraid to eat; counting or restricting calories is counterproductive, especially during this initial phase. If you crave food that isn't keto-approved, eat more real food until you feel full. Still feeling hungry after a meal is a common sign that you are eating too little fat and too much protein.

Another consideration is mineral deficiencies. It's a widespread myth that sodium is bad for us and raises blood pressure. We actually need a whole lot of sodium to survive—not from refined sources, but from sea salt. There's a big difference between refined salt and sea salt; refined salt is found in all kinds of processed foods, and the body considers it to be toxic. Sea salt, on the other hand, is crucial for nerves, muscles, neurological function, and the immune system. Fun fact: You could eat sea salt scoop by scoop and not die from it. Every other substance, including water, can be lethal in high enough doses, but not salt—you would throw up before you came close to your body's limit.

Your body has the capacity to excrete as much as 3½ ounces (100 grams) of sodium per day. Are you rarely thirsty? Do you work out a lot? Do you sweat a lot? Are you getting a lot of refined salt from consuming processed foods? Then it's highly likely that you are running low on sodium. Sodium, magnesium, and potassium are three very important minerals that you can get from natural sources, such as spinach, kale, and avocado (potassium); sea salt (sodium); and pumpkin seeds and mackerel (magnesium). All three minerals affect heart rhythm, pulse, and blood pressure. When levels are too low, they can give rise to psychological symptoms, such as anxiety, nervousness, and food cravings.

One known remedy to tackle food cravings is peppermint oil. You can find peppermint oil at your local whole-foods store. Put a few drops in your tea whenever you crave non-keto food. Peppermint oil is also beneficial for digestive issues, as it has a calming effect on the nervous system.

KEEPING A KETO JOURNAL

I highly recommend that you keep track of your food intake during this initial phase. You don't need to measure anything; just track what you eat to get a general view of your progress. You can also write down how you feel and whether you experience any cravings. It's interesting to see when and why you crave certain foods—for example, if it's because of hunger or stress or because you're feeling low.

PROBLEMS KETO-ADAPTING

The most common reason people don't adapt properly to the ketogenic diet is too much protein and too little fat. Maintain a fat ratio of 60 to 80 percent to avoid this issue.

Other common problems are poor sleep and adrenal stress. A stressful job, a troubled home environment, a sedentary lifestyle, and late hours are all very stressful on the body. Try to get the basics right: go to sleep before 11 p.m., sleep for six to eight hours, and eat breakfast within thirty minutes of waking.

The keto diet is an anti-inflammatory diet, so inflammatory issues will improve with time. I highly recommend the cleansing and detox aids on pages 278 to 280; they are very beneficial for keto-adaptation!

HOW TO TACKLE THE KETO FLU

Constipation, low energy, rash, heart palpitations, and light-headedness generally can be resolved with sea salt, magnesium, and potassium. Magnesium supplements can be very beneficial if you also suffer from leg cramps and persistent constipation.

MEAL PLAN GUIDELINES

This thirty-day meal plan is unlike any other meal plan you might have seen. I'm not going to dictate amounts of food to you. That would be impossible, as keto is a very individualized process. Most people aren't used to listening to their bodies or acting on its signals, but you are going to learn how to do so if you stick to this lifestyle.

Please don't fast, starve, or restrict calories during the introductory phase. There's no need to feel hungry between meals! If you need to, have a snack (see the list, opposite).

KETO-APPROVED SNACKS:

Bone broth

Coconut butter

Coconut milk

Fat bombs

Fatty coffee or tea

Herbal teas

Keto-friendly protein shakes

Macadamia nuts

Olives

See the list of drinks in the general food advice section.

PHASE 1

- Aim for 7 ounces (200 g) of fat per day.

- Limit egg intake to six eggs per day to avoid egg intolerance and stomach upset.

- Limit coconut oil to 1 teaspoon a day to acclimate your body to it.

- Take walks and do very light weight training.

SUGGESTED PREPARATIONS

In advance, buy the following keto-friendly foods:

- Bacon without additives

- Meat (pork, lamb, or beef)

- A few pieces of salmon

- Eggs

- Avocados

- Red and green cabbage

- Broccoli

- Mushrooms

- Onions

- Spinach

- At least ten cans of coconut milk

- A lot of butter

Before you begin the plan, also make a big batch of homemade mayonnaise (page 216) and put it in a jar in the refrigerator, and prepare Keto Burgers (page 148) and a Keto Stew (opposite). These preparations will make everything more convenient during the week.

The Keto Burgers and Keto Stew will keep for more than a week in the refrigerator and even longer in the freezer. If you don't eat the whole batch within a week, place the stew and/or burgers in containers and store them in the freezer until the following week.

KETO *stew*

This stew is so simple that I can hardly call it a recipe, but it's a great dish to get you through the early stages of becoming keto-adapted. It's a mainstay of the meal plan that follows, which is why I've included it here. You can substitute chicken for the pork if you like.

■ Yield: 10 servings   ■ Preparation time: 10 minutes   ■ Cook time: 1 hour

INGREDIENTS

4½ pounds (2 kg) pork tenderloin

Salt and pepper

3 medium yellow onions, chopped

6 cups (1.5 L) coconut milk

3½ ounces (100 g) unsalted butter, plus more for frying

INSTRUCTIONS

■ Cut the pork in 1-inch (2.5-cm) cubes and season with salt and pepper. Fry the onions in some butter in a frying pan over medium heat until golden. Add the seasoned pork and fry until browned on all sides; it will take only a couple of minutes.

■ Transfer the pork and onions to a stew pot. Add the coconut milk and butter and simmer for about 45 minutes. You can leave it on longer if you want the meat more tender, but do not cook it for more than 2 hours.

PHASE 1

	BREAKFAST	LUNCH	DINNER
day 01	Omelet of choice with Mayonnaise and avocado	Keto Burger with butter and Broccoli Mash	Spinach Soup with Boiled Eggs
day 02	Keto Burger with butter and fried eggs	Keto Stew with Broccoli Mash	Spinach Soup with Boiled Eggs
day 03	Breakfast Porridge with butter and cinnamon	Keto Stew with fried spinach	Keto Stew with fried spinach
day 04	Scrambled Eggs with Mayonnaise and avocado	Pan-Fried Salmon Steak with Herb Butter*	Keto Stew with Broccoli Mash
day 05	Boiled eggs with Mayonnaise and fried spinach	Pan-Fried Salmon Steak with Herb Butter	Keto Burger with Coleslaw

Sauce made with coconut cream and butter or heavy cream and butter is okay.

BREAKFAST	LUNCH	DINNER	
Breakfast Porridge with butter and cinnamon (leftover)	Shrimp Omelet with Asparagus (158)	Keto Stew with Cabbage Mash (leftover, 195)	day 06
Bacon and Eggs with Mayonnaise and avocado (140, leftover)	Keto Burger with Broccoli Mash (leftover, leftover)	Pan-Fried Salmon Steak with Herb Butter and Cabbage Mash (168, leftover)	day 07
Breakfast Porridge with butter and cinnamon (130)	Omelet of choice	Keto Stew with Cabbage Mash (leftover, leftover)	day 08
Bacon and Eggs with Mayonnaise and avocado (140, leftover)	Keto Burger with fried spinach (leftover)	Keto Stew with Cauliflower Rice (leftover, 198)	day 09
Bacon and Eggs with Mayonnaise (140, leftover)	Egg and Shrimp Salad or other salad of choice, with extra Mayonnaise (156)	Spinach Soup with Boiled Eggs (154)	day 10

This marks the end of day ten. You have been following a strict and repetitive meal plan to ensure that you get into ketosis without hunger or cravings. I have deliberately kept variations to a minimum. If you are like me and love simplicity and convenience above all else, it's completely fine to eat the stew, spinach, and eggs for the whole period.

Keep track of your progress in your keto journal, and note if you experience an adverse reaction to any of the foods. Some people are sensitive to eggs without knowing it; in that case, omit eggs for a couple of weeks. Be careful with coconut oil on an empty stomach. Don't eat too fast, and never eat standing up. Sit down at a table, not in front of a computer. Chew your food thoroughly. Let it take at least thirty minutes to finish a meal. Set a timer if you need to! If you are a speed eater, your body won't have time to produce enough stomach acids, which will increase your risk of adverse reactions.

PHASE 2

	BREAKFAST	LUNCH	DINNER
day 11	Keto Swedish Pancakes	Keto Burger Pancake Wrap	Keto Stew with steamed vegetables
day 12	Keto Burger with fried spinach	Omelet of choice with avocado	Meat-Filled Bell Pepper with Béarnaise and Broccoli Mash
day 13	Blue Chia Porridge	Keto Stew with Cauliflower Mash	Zucchini Boats with Béarnaise and steamed vegetables
day 14	Scrambled Eggs with Mayonnaise and avocado	Fried fish fillet, preferably mackerel, with herb butter and steamed vegetables	Keto Stew with Broccoli Mash
day 15	Boiled eggs with Mayonnaise and fried spinach	Fried fish fillet, preferably mackerel, with herb butter and steamed vegetables	Keto Burger with Coleslaw

Make a new batch of Mayonnaise, Keto Stew, and Keto Burgers. (Toss a few burgers in the freezer for use in Phase 3 if you don't want to make a third batch later.) These will be your staples in Phase 2 as well. If you substitute the same amount of chicken for pork, you can make a lovely chicken stew. The menu is somewhat similar to the first phase, with a few alterations, such as meat-filled bell peppers, zucchini boats, pancakes, and chia porridge. Salmon is replaced by a fish fillet of your choice. I suggest mackerel, as it helps alleviate keto flu symptoms.

Track your hunger and cravings in your keto journal. In Phase 2 you can skip lunch or dinner, but not breakfast. Continue with light training.

BREAKFAST	LUNCH	DINNER	
Breakfast Porridge with butter and cinnamon	Shrimp Omelet with Asparagus	Keto Stew with Cabbage Mash	day 16
Bacon and Eggs with Mayonnaise and avocado	Keto Burger with Broccoli Mash	Fried fish fillet, preferably mackerel, with herb butter and steamed vegetables	day 17
Breakfast Porridge with butter and cinnamon	Omelet of choice	Keto Stew with Cabbage Mash	day 18
Bacon and Eggs with Mayonnaise and avocado	Keto Burger with fried spinach	Keto Stew with Cauliflower Rice	day 19
Scrambled Eggs with butter and avocado	Egg and Shrimp Salad or other salad of choice, with extra Mayonnaise	Spinach Soup with Boiled Eggs	day 20

Congratulations!

You are almost at the three-week mark! I hope you have noticed some interesting changes in your body. If you are suffering from the keto flu, know that it will pass in a few weeks or less. If you are suffering from keto rash, know that it is your Candida (yeast infections) dying off. They can be persistent, but you're doing what it takes to clear yourself of them. Candida and the keto diet cannot coexist for long! Whatever you do, steer clear of antibiotics.

PHASE 3

	BREAKFAST	LUNCH	DINNER
day 21	Breakfast Porridge with butter and cinnamon — 130	Fried fish fillet with Marinated Vegetables — 204	Keto Stew with steamed vegetables — 117
day 22	Keto Burger with fried spinach — 148	Omelet of choice with avocado	Meat-Filled Keto Tortilla with Guacamole and salad of choice — 180 / 188
day 23	Blue Chia Porridge — 131	Shrimp Omelet with Asparagus — 158	Steak with Béarnaise and Cabbage Mash — 184 / 195
day 24	Scrambled Eggs with Mayonnaise and avocado — 141 / leftover	Creamy Salmon Soup — 155	Keto Stew with Broccoli Mash — leftover / leftover
day 25	Boiled eggs with Mayonnaise and fried spinach — leftover	Pan-Fried Salmon Steak with Herb Butter — 168	Keto Burger with Coleslaw — leftover / leftover

This is the final phase of the plan. Now you are free to substitute other recipes as long as they follow the keto guidelines. I suggest that you stick to the breakfast routine and light training for a few more weeks. After that, if you feel great and want to try specific types of fasting, go ahead, as long as you feel good and have sufficient energy!

BREAKFAST	LUNCH	DINNER	
leftover Breakfast Porridge with butter and cinnamon	158 Shrimp Omelet with Asparagus	leftover leftover Keto Stew with Cabbage Mash	day **26**
140 leftover Bacon and Eggs with Mayonnaise and avocado	Fried fish fillet with herb butter and steamed vegetables	174 Creamy Mussels with Sautéed Spinach	day **27**
leftover Breakfast Porridge with butter and cinnamon	Omelet of choice	leftover leftover Keto Stew with Cabbage Mash	day **28**
140 leftover Bacon and Eggs with Mayonnaise and avocado	leftover Keto Burger with fried spinach	leftover leftover Keto Stew with Cauliflower Rice	day **29**
141 Scrambled Eggs with butter and avocado	Salad of choice (such as tuna, egg, or shrimp) with extra Mayonnaise	182 Keto Pizza	day **30**

This is the end of the thirty-day period, but I hope you feel inspired to continue. Stick to simple food choices and experiment with different food amounts, fat ratios, and meal intervals. The keto diet is filled with aha moments, because there's always more to learn about the body. You are on the fast track toward healing, so you will see weight loss and other positive side effects in due time; stay patient and don't second-guess your body's ability to heal itself.

Best of luck!

RECIPES

BREAKFAST

Breakfast is usually the hardest meal to keto-adjust, especially for beginners. Many people grew up with carb-based breakfasts consisting of foods like toast, cereal, egg sandwiches, sweetened yogurt, and orange juice. We are programmed to think of breakfast as something entirely different from dinner, but what most keto enthusiasts come to realize after a while is that it is completely fine to swap meals around or even skip meals. When you eliminate all foods that affect insulin and blood sugar, it's not uncommon to crave real foods like eggs, meat, and fish upon waking in the morning.

This section provides you with some keto-friendly breakfast options.

KETO SWEDISH *pancakes*

Swedish-style pancakes are larger and thinner than American pancakes, and we generally smear them with butter, roll them up, and eat them with a knife and fork. You can also eat them with whipped cream and berries, but they work equally well as cold wraps or crepes.

In this recipe, I share my favorite weekend breakfast that is perfect for a day off. I make these pancakes whenever my husband and I can have breakfast together without needing to rush off to work.

■ Yield: Ten 8-inch (20-cm) pancakes ■ Preparation time: 15 to 20 minutes

INGREDIENTS

BATTER:

8 large eggs

1/3 cup (80 ml) coconut flour

1/4 cup (60 ml) flax meal

3 tablespoons unsalted butter, melted, plus more for the pan

FOR SERVING (optional):

Fresh berries

Heavy cream or coconut cream

INSTRUCTIONS

■ Put all the batter ingredients in a bowl and mix well with an electric mixer until smooth and fluffy.

■ Heat a small (8-inch [20-cm]) frying pan over medium heat. If you have an even smaller frying pan, use that one! The smaller the pan, the easier it will be to make great-looking pancakes. Add 1/2 tablespoon of butter to the pan for each pancake to ensure that it doesn't stick. The pancakes are ready to flip when they are golden and stick together. Be careful when turning, and make sure to watch the pancakes the entire time.

Quick CREPES

You can make 4 delicious crepes or thin pancakes in a matter of seconds just by combining eggs and cream cheese. Here's a quick recipe!

■ Yield: Four 8-inch (20-cm) pancakes ■ Preparation time: 5 minutes

INGREDIENTS

2 large eggs

2 ounces (55 g) cream cheese

4 teaspoons unsalted butter, divided

INSTRUCTIONS

■ Put the eggs and cream cheese in a blender and blend until smooth. Heat an 8-inch (20-cm) frying pan over medium heat. When hot, melt 1 teaspoon of butter in the pan, then pour one-quarter of the batter into the pan. Cook until golden brown on both sides, about 1 minute per side depending on your type of stove. Repeat with the rest of the batter.

BREAKFAST
porridge

It's a deep-seated tradition in Nordic countries to start the day with a big bowl of porridge. Most kids eat porridge for breakfast and continue to do so into adulthood. This porridge is completely dairy-free, keto-approved, very satiating, and absolutely delicious. It's a definite go-to whenever you need some extra fuel.

■ Yield: 2 servings ■ Preparation time: 2 minutes ■ Cook time: 5 to 7 minutes

INGREDIENTS

3 large eggs

1 cup (240 ml) coconut cream

2 tablespoons coconut flour

1 tablespoon coconut oil

TOPPINGS (optional):

Coconut flakes

Ground cinnamon

Unsalted butter

INSTRUCTIONS

■ Put all the ingredients in a frying pan over high heat and stir vigorously while the eggs heat up, making sure the mixture doesn't boil or burn. It takes only a few minutes for the porridge to be ready, so keep watching and stirring the entire time. Serve with toppings, if desired.

keto tip

You can replace the coconut cream with dairy-based heavy cream or even water; see what works best for you.

BLUE CHIA *porridge*

This porridge contains chia seeds, and they take some time to swell. To make sure that the porridge thickens by breakfast time, prepare it the night before.

■ Yield: 4 servings   ■ Preparation time: 5 minutes, plus 4 hours to chill

INGREDIENTS

2 cups (480 ml) coconut milk or coconut cream

½ cup (120 g) fresh or frozen blueberries, plus extra for garnish

5¾ ounces (80 g) chia seeds (black or white)

15 drops liquid stevia

½ teaspoon ground cinnamon or 1 teaspoon vanilla extract (optional)

Coconut flakes, for garnish (optional)

INSTRUCTIONS

■ Place all the ingredients in a blender and blend for 2 minutes, until completely smooth. Pour the mixture into one large or four small containers and refrigerate for at least 4 hours to let it gel. It will keep in the refrigerator for at least 5 days.

■ When the porridge is ready, it will be thick and creamy. It can be eaten cold, but it tastes a lot better and is more satiating when hot. Microwave on high for 1 minute, take it out, and stir to make sure it's hot enough.

■ Enjoy this porridge just as it is or top it with extra blueberries and coconut flakes.

KETO *"breads"*

Bread is something that a lot of people miss on the keto diet, but it's generally one of the unhealthiest and most fattening foods out there. Regular bread contains gluten and yeast, which irritate the gut lining and lead to cravings, hunger, and bloating. Unfortunately, many gluten-free, low-carb, and even keto-friendly alternatives are not the best choices for weight loss. Don't make keto bread the basis of your diet; eat it sparingly and focus on complete meals as much as possible.

KETO *crispbread*

Crispbread is a traditional Nordic bread that is commonly consumed with boiled eggs and caviar. This keto-friendly version can serve as the base for any topping or spread, but I like to eat it with a slather of butter and nothing else. It's free of gluten, dairy, eggs, and lactose but can be irritating to sensitive stomachs. That is why the seeds are soaked beforehand; soaking seeds makes them a lot easier on the gut!

■ Yield: Forty 3-inch (7.5-cm) squares   ■ Preparation time: 15 minutes, plus 8 hours to soak seeds
■ Cook time: 2 hours

INGREDIENTS

¾ cup (180 ml) sesame seeds

¼ cup plus 3 tablespoons (100 ml) flax seeds

1 cup (240 ml) sunflower seeds

2 cups (480 ml) water

¼ cup plus 3 tablespoons (100 ml) almond flour

¼ cup (60 ml) ground psyllium husks

1 teaspoon salt

INSTRUCTIONS

■ To soak the seeds, put the sesame seeds and flax seeds in a large bowl; the seeds will likely swell to double their size or more, so make sure to choose a bowl that allows plenty of room for swelling. Add enough water to cover the seeds and soak for 6 hours. To the same bowl, add the sunflower seeds and more water, if needed, and let soak for another 2 hours. Make sure the seeds are completely covered with water at all times.

■ Preheat the oven to 220°F (105°C). Line two rimmed baking sheets with parchment paper and brush some oil on the paper. (Any keto cooking oil will do.)

■ Drain and rinse the seeds and place them in a mixing bowl, then add the water, almond flour, psyllium husks, and salt. Mix the ingredients together and set aside for a couple of minutes to thicken. Spread the thick mixture on the prepared baking sheets and bake for 2 hours, until hard and crispy. If you make the crispbread too thick, it might turn out a bit softer, but it will still be delicious! Cut the crispbread into pieces while still hot from the oven and let it cool before unpanning.

■ The crispbread will keep for a month if stored in a cool, dry place.

CLASSIC OOPSIES
with a twist

This bread has been around since the early 1970s, having originated in Dr. Robert Atkins' book The Diet Revolution. *It doesn't have a lot of flavor, so you will need a nice topping or spread. You can also use these breads as hamburger buns. The original recipe is just eggs, salt, and cream cheese, but I've added baking powder and psyllium husk, hence the twist. This makes the Oopsies more bread-like.*

■ Yield: 6 to 8 breads ■ Preparation time: 10 minutes ■ Cook time: 25 minutes

INGREDIENTS

3 large eggs

Pinch of salt

4 ounces (100 g) cream cheese, softened

1 tablespoon ground psyllium husks

½ teaspoon baking powder

1½ teaspoons sesame seeds, for garnish

tip

You can omit the psyllium husks and baking powder; you will still have Oopsies, just not as breadlike.

INSTRUCTIONS

■ Preheat the oven to 300°F (150°C). Line a baking sheet with parchment paper, then brush some cooking oil on the paper. (Any keto cooking oil will do.)

■ Separate the eggs, putting the whites in a clean, dry medium-sized mixing bowl and the yolks in a larger bowl. Add the salt to the whites and whip with an electric mixer until stiff peaks form; you should be able to turn the bowl upside down and the whites won't slide out.

■ Put the cream cheese in the bowl with the yolks and use the electric mixer to mix them together until smooth, then add the psyllium husks and baking powder and mix to combine.

■ Gently fold the egg whites into the egg yolk mixture, using a spatula to work the whites evenly into the yolk mixture while keeping the whites as fluffy as possible.

■ Using a large spoon, scoop 6 large or 8 smaller portions of the dough onto a baking sheet, spaced 2 to 3 inches (5 to 7.5 cm) apart. Sprinkle the sesame seeds on top and bake for 25 minutes, until they turn golden. For best flavor, serve hot from the oven. Leftovers will keep for a week when stored in a cool, dry place.

YOGURT *breakfast*

Yogurt is another classic breakfast alternative that typically doesn't go well with the keto diet because of the dairy protein's insulinemic effects on the body. Even high-fat yogurt can impede ketosis, so I highly suggest a dairy-free approach if weight loss is your number-one goal. Dairy-free yogurt that is low in carbohydrates can work, though. Here, I show you how to make your own. Some natural foods stores sell this kind of yogurt, but it's fairly simple to make it yourself!

Dairy-free PROBIOTIC YOGURT

This dairy-free yogurt has the sour taste of real yogurt. All you need is coconut milk and a good probiotic supplement. When choosing a probiotic, make sure it's a brand with at least ten different bacterial strains and a minimum of two billion bacteria per dose. Supplements come in capsule and liquid form; the form you choose doesn't matter much for this recipe.

■ Yield: 6 to 8 servings   ■ Preparation time: 5 minutes, plus 2 to 3 days to cultivate

INGREDIENTS

2 cups (480 ml) coconut milk

3 to 4 probiotic capsules (6 to 8 billion probiotics total)

note ───────

If the yogurt gets a weird taste or smell, throw it out. It means that contamination has occurred, and bacteria other than the good ones are brewing in your yogurt!

INSTRUCTIONS

■ It's important to use a clean, non-metallic bowl. Glass is ideal, but plastic or ceramic is fine, too. Put the coconut milk in the bowl and whisk with a non-metal tool until fluffy.

■ Open the probiotic capsules and pour the contents into the milk. Place a clean towel over the bowl and leave it on the counter to ferment for 2 to 3 days. Once a day, stir and taste the yogurt with a clean, dry spoon. When it has the level of sourness you like, it's done. Put the yogurt in the refrigerator to inhibit further cultivation of the probiotic bacteria. It will keep in the fridge for up to a week.

GRANOLA

This granola is delicious with Dairy-Free Probiotic Yogurt (page 136) and also with porridge (pages 130 and 131).

■ Yield: 2 heaping cups (500 ml)　■ Preparation time: 5 minutes　■ Cook time: 20 minutes

INGREDIENTS

1 large egg white

3 ounces (100 g) raw almonds, finely chopped

3 ounces (100 g) raw pecans, finely chopped

3½ ounces (100 g) unsweetened coconut flakes

3½ ounces (60 g) sesame seeds

2½ ounces (30 g) almond flour

2½ teaspoons ginger powder

Pinch of salt

4 tablespoons (55 g) unsalted butter, softened

INSTRUCTIONS

- Preheat the oven to 300°F (150°C).

- In a bowl, whisk the egg white with an electric mixer until stiff peaks form. Stir in the almonds, pecans, coconut flakes, sesame seeds, almond flour, ginger powder, and salt, then add the butter with your fingers. Work the mixture until it looks like a dough and clumps together.

- Line a rimmed baking sheet with parchment paper and crumble the granola over it. Bake for 20 minutes, keeping an eye on the granola to make sure it doesn't burn.

- Store the granola in the refrigerator in a tightly sealed jar for up to a month. Because it contains fat, it will not stay crispy at room temperature.

Eggs are super-healthy and contain almost every nutrient we need, which makes them a great breakfast. If you have a sensitive stomach and get bloated from eating eggs, it's probably the whites that are causing the problem. Try removing the whites and eating just the yolks to see how you tolerate them. The yolks are basically just fat and nutrients.

BACON AND EGGS

I ate bacon and eggs frequently while I was experimenting with ketosis. It's safe to say that you can't go wrong with this classic breakfast. This is exactly the type of food that will put you in ketosis in no time!

■Yield: 1 serving   ■Preparation time: 2 minutes   ■Cook time: 10 minutes

INGREDIENTS

5 slices bacon

2 large eggs

Salt

INSTRUCTIONS

■ In a frying pan, fry the bacon over medium heat, then remove the bacon to a plate and fry the eggs in the bacon fat. If you are using pasteurized eggs, leave the yolks a bit runny; a hard white and a softer yolk maximize the nutritional value. Serve immediately, sprinkled with salt.

SCRAMBLED EGGS

This is another favorite that is too great not to include in this collection of keto-friendly breakfasts.

■ Yield: 1 serving　　■ Preparation time: 2 minutes　　■ Cook time: 8 minutes

INGREDIENTS

2 large eggs

1 tablespoon coconut cream, crème fraîche, or Egg Milk (page 244)

1 tablespoon unsalted butter, plus more for serving

Salt

INSTRUCTIONS

■ Put the eggs, coconut cream, and butter in a frying pan over medium-low heat. Cook, stirring with a spatula from the sides to the middle to "scramble" the eggs. If you like your scrambled eggs soft and creamy, remove the pan from the heat when some of the egg is still liquid-y and let the residual heat of the pan finish cooking them. Serve when you are satisfied with the texture, and enjoy with a good amount of butter and a sprinkle of salt!

tip

To make super-creamy scrambled eggs, cook the eggs in a heatproof bowl set on top of a saucepan of simmering water (don't let the bottom of the bowl touch the water), stirring often.

SAVORY MUSHROOM *omelet*

An easy open-faced omelet—no flipping needed!

■ Yield: 1 serving   ■ Preparation time: 8 minutes   ■ Cook time: 10 minutes

INGREDIENTS

1½ ounces (50 g) mushrooms, sliced

½ red or yellow onion, sliced

Unsalted butter, for the pan

2 large eggs, lightly whisked

½ cup (120 ml) coconut cream or heavy cream

Salt and pepper

serving tip
Serve with homemade mayonnaise (page 216).

INSTRUCTIONS

■ In a medium-sized frying pan (preferably nonstick) over medium heat, fry the mushrooms and onion in some butter until soft and golden, about 8 minutes. Reduce the heat to low, add the eggs and cream, and stir with a spatula to make sure the ingredients are well combined. Cook until the omelet is set and done to your liking. An omelet is best when it's soft and creamy, so take it off the heat when the eggs look ready; don't let the omelet burn! Season with salt and pepper and serve.

keto tip
Mushrooms are keto-approved and well tolerated by almost everyone. Onions can be a bit hard on the stomach, though, so if you are sensitive to them or you suffer from an autoimmune disorder, leave them out of this dish.

AVOCADO BAKED EGGS

■Yield: 2 servings   ■Preparation time: 5 minutes   ■Cook time: 20 minutes

INGREDIENTS

2 ripe avocados

4 large eggs

Salt and pepper

serving tip ———

Sprinkle bacon bits or grated cheese on top and serve with mayonnaise (page 216) on the side.

INSTRUCTIONS

■ Preheat the oven to 425°F (220°C).

■ Cut the avocados in half and remove the pits. Crack the eggs into a bowl, keeping the yolks intact, and spoon one yolk into each avocado hole. Continue spooning in some of the whites until the avocado is full. Season each with a pinch of salt and pepper, then bake for about 20 minutes, until the eggs are fully set.

LUNCH

When following a keto diet, you will experience hunger and satiation without the impact of blood sugar and insulin. This will affect your eating habits and make you want to eat fewer meals. Most keto dieters don't snack, for example, and some skip breakfast and/or lunch. Few people skip dinner, though. Personally, I tend to eat at unusual times, like having dinner at 3 p.m. Breakfast and dinner are my two musts in a day.

This section includes eighteen different meal suggestions divided into lunch and dinner. If you want to have a lunch alternative for dinner or vice versa, that's totally fine!

KETO BURGERS

These burgers are a perfect choice for any lunch box; they are good cold or heated up. Just add garlic butter and the sides of your choice. In the photo, opposite, I paired the burgers with Pumpkin Wedges (page 202) and Cauliflower Mash (page 194) made with a head of purple cauliflower to make it more colorful.

Keto burgers will keep in the refrigerator for more than a week and freeze well, so this recipe makes a big batch.

■ Yield: 14 servings ■ Preparation time: 10 minutes ■ Cook time: about 30 minutes

INGREDIENTS

4¾ pounds (2.2 kg) ground pork or ground beef, or a blend

4 large egg yolks

Salt and pepper

Unsalted butter, for frying

note

Omit the egg yolks from this recipe if you are sensitive to eggs or follow an autoimmune protocol.

INSTRUCTIONS

■ In a large bowl, use your hands to mix together the ground meat and egg yolks. Form the mixture into 14 patties. Sprinkle salt and pepper on both sides of the patties, then fry them in a good amount of butter in a large frying pan over medium heat. (To save time, use two or three frying pans at once.) Make sure that they are fully and evenly cooked before eating; cut one in half to see if it's ready. (If making all-beef patties, cook the burgers until at least medium done [150°F/65°C or higher]; if cooking all-pork patties or a blend of pork and beef, cook them until medium to medium-well done [160°F/71°C or higher].)

PANCAKE WRAPS

■ The pancakes on page 128 and the crepes on page 129 make great wraps for these burgers. I fill my wraps with lettuce, homemade mayonnaise (page 216), and a burger.

■ The wraps will keep in the refrigerator for up to 3 days, so you can prepare a batch in advance for your lunch box.

SHIRATAKI PESTO *noodles*

Most products with "low carb" printed across the packaging should be avoided because they are made with artificial ingredients or are not low-carb at all. One exception to this rule is Japanese shirataki noodles, a translucent, gelatinous product made from water and glucomannan.

Glucomannan is a water-soluble dietary fiber with almost zero carbs and calories—and unfortunately very little flavor. But that makes shirataki noodles the perfect neutral vehicle for many keto sauces! I find shirataki noodles to be the best substitute for pasta. They usually come in water-filled plastic containers; discard this liquid before cooking. If you want the noodles to be more similar to pasta, you can dry-roast them.

■Yield: 1 serving ■Preparation time: 1 minute ■Cook time: 1 to 3 minutes

INGREDIENTS

1 (7-ounce/200-g) package shirataki noodles

¼ cup (60 ml) pesto, homemade (page 190) or store-bought

INSTRUCTIONS

- *To dry-roast the noodles,* discard the water from the package and put the noodles in a dry frying pan. Fry over high heat for 1 minute, stirring often. When they make a slight squeaking noise when you move them around in the pan, they're ready.

- *To boil the noodles,* bring a pot of water to a boil. Discard the water from the package and add the noodles to the boiling water. Boil for 3 minutes, then drain.

- Toss the noodles with the pesto and serve. It's one of the fastest meals you can make!

VARIATION

- If you don't like pesto or can't consume it because it contains pine nuts, try tossing the noodles in your favorite pasta sauce with some ground meat.

ZUCCHINI BOATS

■Yield: 2 servings   ■Preparation time: 15 minutes   ■Cook time: 30 minutes

INGREDIENTS

2 small (7- to 8-inch/20-cm) or 1 large (12-inch/30-cm) zucchini

1 pound (455 g) ground meat

2 tablespoons unsalted butter

½ yellow onion, finely chopped

3 tablespoons tomato sauce

1½ ounces (50 g) mushrooms, sliced

1 small tomato, sliced

Salt and pepper

INSTRUCTIONS

■ Preheat the oven to 300°F (150°C).

■ Peel the zucchini and cut them in half lengthwise. Remove the seeds and scrape out the middle to make room for the filling. Place on a rimmed baking sheet or in a small baking dish.

■ In a frying pan over medium heat, fry the ground meat with the butter, onion, and tomato sauce, stirring to break up the meat into small clumps, until the meat is no longer pink, about 6 minutes. Add the mushrooms and tomato slices to the pan and cook until they are softened, 4 to 5 minutes.

■ Fill the zucchini with the filling and bake for 15 to 20 minutes, until the zucchini are tender.

VARIATION

■ Top the filling with ½ cup (120 ml) of shredded cheese and let it melt in the oven.

SPINACH SOUP *with* *boiled eggs*

This simple lunch is loaded with nutrients and serves as a great biohack to cure hangovers! It restores many of the minerals, such as potassium, that are depleted with alcohol intake. If you can't consume eggs, just omit them; this recipe is equally good without them.

■ Yield: 2 servings ■ Preparation time: 15 minutes ■ Cook time: 12 minutes

INGREDIENTS

1 (1-pound/455-g) package frozen spinach, defrosted

3 tablespoons unsalted butter

4 large eggs

½ cup (120 ml) coconut cream

Salt and pepper

INSTRUCTIONS

■ Put the spinach and butter in a saucepan over medium-low heat. Cover and simmer for 10 minutes. Meanwhile, in another saucepan, boil the eggs for 8 minutes.

■ Remove the eggs from the heat, rinse in cold water, then peel them and cut them in half.

■ Add the cream and a pinch each of salt and pepper to the spinach, stir, and simmer for 1 to 2 minutes. Pour into two serving bowls and add two eggs to each bowl.

CREAMY SALMON *soup*

This lovely and nutritious soup is quick and easy to make. This recipe calls for poaching the salmon, but you can also pan-fry it to give it more texture (as shown in the photo). To pan-fry the salmon, follow the frying method on page 168, then cut the salmon into squares.

■Yield: 2 servings ■Preparation time: 5 minutes ■Cook time: 12 minutes

INGREDIENTS

9 ounces (255 g) fresh or frozen salmon fillets or steaks, defrosted if frozen

1 cup (240 ml) coconut cream

2 tablespoons unsalted butter

Salt and pepper

INSTRUCTIONS

■ Cut the salmon into squares. Bring a saucepan of water to a simmer, then add the salmon and simmer for 10 minutes, making sure not to overcook the fish. Drain, then return the salmon to the saucepan.

■ Add the coconut cream and butter to the saucepan with the salmon and season with salt and pepper. Bring to a simmer and let simmer for 2 minutes, then serve.

EGG AND SHRIMP *salad*

A salad is always a refreshing option and can be varied endlessly. Be careful with ready-made dressings and vinaigrettes, which can contain a lot of sugar, even if they don't taste sweet at all. I stick to my homemade mayonnaise (page 216) when it comes to salad; that way I know it won't kick me out of ketosis.

■ Yield: 1 serving   ■ Preparation time: 10 minutes   ■ Cook time: 12 minutes

INGREDIENTS

3 large eggs

3½ ounces (100 g) peeled medium shrimp, defrosted if frozen

⅓ medium red onion, finely chopped

Unsalted butter, for frying

1 small tomato, diced (optional)

Leaves from 1 (6-inch/ 15-cm) head of lettuce

½ avocado, diced, or 10 pitted black olives

Sugar-free dressing or vinaigrette or homemade mayonnaise (page 216)

INSTRUCTIONS

■ Boil the eggs for 8 minutes. Rinse in cold water, then peel and slice the eggs.

■ Fry the shrimp and onion in butter over medium heat until the shrimp is opaque and the onion has softened, 4 to 5 minutes. Put the tomatoes, if using, in a bowl with the lettuce leaves. Add the eggs, shrimp and onion, and avocado or olives and drizzle some dressing on top.

tip

The eggs, tomatoes, and onions may be replaced with broccoli, cauliflower, and green beans if you have an immune disorder or follow an AIP protocol.

SHRIMP OMELET
with
asparagus

There are no strict rules when it comes to omelets. The base is always eggs and cream, either dairy cream or coconut cream—the rest is up to you. You can experiment with different types of mushrooms, onions, spices, and even proteins like tuna, shrimp, or chicken. My personal favorite is this shrimp omelet with asparagus.

■ Yield: 1 serving ■ Preparation time: 8 minutes ■ Cook time: 13 minutes

INGREDIENTS

¹/₃ medium red onion

2 mushrooms (optional)

Unsalted butter, for frying

3½ ounces (100 g) peeled medium shrimp, defrosted if frozen

3 large eggs

¹/₃ cup (80 ml) heavy cream or coconut cream

7 ounces (200 g) asparagus

Salt and pepper

Chopped fresh basil, for garnish (optional)

INSTRUCTIONS

■ In a medium-sized frying pan (preferably nonstick) over medium heat, fry the onion and mushrooms in some butter until soft and golden, about 8 minutes. Add the shrimp and fry for 2 minutes, while stirring. Reduce the heat to low, add the eggs and cream, and stir with a spatula until the eggs are just set and still moist. Season with salt and pepper to taste. Move the omelet to a plate.

■ In the same frying pan, fry the asparagus in butter over high heat for 3 minutes, until crisp-tender. Add the asparagus to the plate with the omelet, garnish with basil, if desired, and serve.

Moist and tender CHICKEN BREAST

Chicken is a great staple for quick lunches, but it needs added fat to qualify as keto; otherwise it's too high in protein and too low in fat. The solution is to serve it with a condiment such as homemade mayonnaise (page 216) or pesto (page 190) or drizzle it with olive oil or an interesting vinaigrette.

Most people tend to overcook chicken so that it's dry rather than succulent. The secret to moist and juicy chicken is to let it soak in a brine for a minimum of 15 minutes. I've included two methods for cooking the brined chicken: boiling and pan-frying. Both work well, but boiling is faster.

■ Yield: 1 serving   ■ Preparation time: 5 minutes, plus at least 15 minutes to brine   ■ Cook time: 15 minutes

INGREDIENTS

1 boneless, skinless chicken breast half (about 8 ounces/225 g)

1 quart (1 L) water

¼ cup (60 ml) salt

Ground black pepper, thyme, or other herbs or spices (optional)

Coconut oil (if pan-frying)

INSTRUCTIONS

■ Put the chicken in a container. Mix the water with the salt until it is dissolved to make a brine. Add some black pepper and other spices to the brine if you like. Pour the brine over the chicken so that the chicken is completely submerged. Place the container in the refrigerator and let the chicken brine for 15 minutes to 4 hours.

■ Remove the chicken from the brine and discard the brine.

■ *To boil the chicken,* put the chicken in a saucepan and cover with fresh water. Bring it to a boil and continue to boil until the chicken is fully cooked and no longer pink in the center, about 15 minutes.

■ *To pan-fry the chicken,* heat up a frying pan over medium-high heat. Meanwhile, pat the excess moisture from the chicken with a paper towel. When the pan is hot, add a teaspoon or two of coconut oil (enough to coat the bottom of the pan well). When the oil is hot, place the chicken in the pan and sear for 1 minute, then flip and sear on the other side for 1 minute. Reduce the heat to low, cover the pan with a lid, and cook for 25 minutes. Check the center of the chicken; if any pink remains, continue cooking, checking for doneness every 5 minutes.

SERVING OPTIONS

■ Chop the chicken into pieces and eat it with a condiment or dressing that is rich in fat (see above).

MOIST AND TENDER CHICKEN BREAST
with beet salad

A salad with boiled chicken and beets makes a great lunch. When the chicken and beets are cooked ahead, it's a quick meal to throw together. Beets are rich in important nutrients like vitamin C, potassium, and manganese. Beets can lower blood pressure and support the liver, kidneys, and pancreas.

■Yield: 1 serving   ■Prep time: 10 minutes   ■Cook time: 1 hour

INGREDIENTS

1 large beet

1 boneless, skinless chicken breast half (about 8 ounces/225 g)

A few handfuls of baby kale leaves

Salt

Sugar-free vinaigrette of choice

INSTRUCTIONS

■ Place the beet in a saucepan of water, bring to a boil, and continue boiling until it can easily be pierced with a knife, about 1 hour.

■ Meanwhile, brine the chicken and pan-fry it until cooked through, following the method on page 160. Chop the chicken into bite-sized pieces.

■ When the beet is done, drain and run cold water over it. When cool enough to handle, peel and chop the beet into bite-sized pieces.

■ Put the kale on a plate and top with the beets and chicken. Season with salt and drizzle with the vinaigrette.

CHICKEN LETTUCE WRAP

Lettuce wraps are an excellent and variable lunch. Besides chicken breast, you can use Tuna Pâté (page 218), a chicken burger or a few chicken meatballs (page 166), and Tomato-Olive Spread (page 217) as a filler, together with the vegetables of your choice and dressing or mayonnaise. I use mayonnaise for this chicken wrap.

■ Yield: 1 serving   ■ Preparation time: 10 minutes (not including time to cook chicken or make mayo)

INGREDIENTS

1 boneless, skinless chicken breast half (about 8 ounces/225 g), brined and boiled or pan-fried (see page 160)

1 large lettuce leaf

Tomato slices

Avocado slices

Mayonnaise (page 216)

Salt and pepper

INSTRUCTIONS

■ Place the cooked chicken breast in the center of the lettuce leaf. Top with tomato and avocado slices and a dollop of mayonnaise. Season to taste with salt and pepper. Wrap the lettuce around the fillings and serve!

■ The wrap will keep for up to 3 days in the refrigerator, so it's safe to store in a lunch box.

VARIATIONS

■ Use ground chicken instead of a plain chicken breast and make a chicken burger for the wrap. You can also fry some vegetables such as onions and mushrooms and add them to your wrap.

CHICKEN BURGERS
or meatballs

■Yield: 4 servings ■Preparation time: 10 minutes ■Cook time: 30 minutes

INGREDIENTS

1 pound (455 g) ground chicken

2 large egg yolks

1/3 cup (80 ml) heavy cream or coconut cream

Pinch of salt and pepper

Unsalted butter, for frying

note ——————

Omit the egg yolks from this recipe if you are sensitive to eggs or follow an autoimmune protocol.

INSTRUCTIONS

■ Put the chicken in a bowl and add the egg yolks and cream. Season with salt and pepper. Combine with your hands until smooth.

■ *To make burgers,* form the mixture into four 3-inch (7-cm) patties. *To make meatballs,* form the mixture into 1-inch (2.5-cm) balls to make a total of 8 to 10 meatballs.
Fry the burgers or meatballs in butter in a frying pan over medium heat for 30 minutes, until fully and evenly cooked through.

SERVING TIPS

■ These burgers work well in lettuce wraps or pancake wraps (page 129), or you can use Oopsies (page 134) as buns.

■ The meatballs can be eaten with shirataki noodles in tomato sauce (shown below). Boil the noodles for 3 minutes, discard the water, add tomato sauce, and toss to coat the noodles.

PAN-FRIED SALMON STEAK *with* *herb butter*

Wild-caught salmon and pink, or humpback, salmon are healthier alternatives to farmed salmon. Salmon is so rich in flavor and nutrients that you don't need any sides except a nice herb butter!

■Yield: 1 serving   ■Preparation time: 5 minutes   ■Cook time: 12 minutes

INGREDIENTS

1 salmon steak (about 9 ounces/255 g), fresh or frozen, defrosted if frozen

2 tablespoons unsalted butter, softened, plus more for frying

1 clove garlic, pressed

1½ teaspoons finely chopped fresh basil, lemon balm, or other herbs of choice

½ lemon

INSTRUCTIONS

■ In a frying pan over medium heat, fry the salmon in butter for 6 minutes on each side, until the fish is opaque in the center and flakes easily. A piece thicker than 1 inch (2.5 cm) may require longer cooking; make sure that the fish is fully cooked through before serving.

■ To make the herb butter, mix the butter with the pressed garlic and some chopped basil leaves, lemon balm leaves, or other fresh herbs you have on hand.

■ Squeeze the lemon over the salmon before eating, and serve with the herb butter on the side.

DINNER

Meat-filled
BELL PEPPERS

■Yield: 4 servings ■Preparation time: 10 minutes ■Cook time: 45 minutes

INGREDIENTS

FILLING:

1/3 cup (80 ml) chopped yellow onions

2 baby portobello (aka cremini) mushrooms, sliced

Unsalted butter, for frying

1 pound (455 g) ground meat

1/2 cup (120 ml) coconut cream

3 tablespoons tomato sauce or salsa

1 small tomato, cut into eighths

Salt and pepper

4 bell peppers, any color

Shredded cheese of choice, for topping (optional)

INSTRUCTIONS

■ Preheat the oven to 300°F (150°C).

■ Make the filling: Fry the onions and mushrooms in some butter in a frying pan over medium heat until tender, about 7 minutes. Add the ground meat and, stirring continuously, pour in the coconut cream and tomato sauce. Add the tomato and fry until cooked through, stirring often to break up the meat into small clumps. Season with salt and pepper.

■ Cut the "lids" off the bell peppers and remove the seeds. Fill the peppers with the meat filling, top with cheese, if using, and bake for 30 minutes, until the cheese is melted and golden. Note: If you like your pepper super-soft, par-boil them in water for 5 minutes before filling them and putting them in the oven.

CREAMY MUSSELS
with sautéed spinach

■ Yield: 4 servings   ■ Preparation time: 5 minutes   ■ Cook time: 20 minutes

INGREDIENTS

20 mussels (about 1 pound/455 g; see tips)

1 clove garlic, finely chopped

1 yellow onion, chopped

1 tablespoon coconut oil

2 cups (480 ml) coconut milk or coconut cream

7 ounces (200 g) fresh or frozen spinach, defrosted if frozen

Pinch of salt and pepper

3 tablespoons unsalted butter

INSTRUCTIONS

■ Pick over the mussels and discard any with cracked shells or shells that are not tightly closed. Scrub and debeard the mussels. To debeard the muscles, find the bristly material sticking out from one side (the "beard"), and remove it by pulling it down and outward toward the hinge of the shell. Boil the mussels in water for 15 minutes or until they open. Discard any mussels that did not open, then remove the mussels from the shells and discard the shells.

■ In a large frying pan over medium heat, sauté the garlic and onion in the coconut oil until fragrant. Add the coconut milk, spinach, and salt and pepper and simmer for 5 minutes. Add the mussels and butter, stir to combine, and remove from the heat. Serve in bowls.

taste tip

For a more mature taste, add ½ cup (120 ml) dry (low-sugar) white wine, such as Sauvignon Blanc, to the mixture. You can garnish the dish with some chopped fresh parsley and lemon balm; it's a great combination of flavors.

tips

Farm-raised mussels will likely come debearded, saving you a step, and will likely not require a vigorous scrubbing, just a good rinsing.

It's always a good idea to add some broth or stock to a dish like this for extra nutrients. To incorporate broth into this recipe, replace 1 cup (240 ml) of the coconut milk with homemade chicken broth (page 286).

Colorful
FISH STEW

■ Yield: 4 servings ■ Preparation time: 5 minutes (not including time to make rice) ■ Cook time: 15 minutes

INGREDIENTS

1 (1-pound/455-g) frozen whitefish fillet, defrosted

4 tablespoons (55 g) unsalted butter, divided

1 quart (1 L) water

1 tablespoon curry powder

2 medium tomatoes, cut into eighths

2 hard-boiled eggs, sliced

Pinch of salt

2 tablespoons chopped fresh parsley

1 batch Cauliflower Rice (page 198), for serving

INSTRUCTIONS

■ Put a tablespoon of the butter in a large frying pan; when the butter is hot, add the fish. Cook for a few minutes, then add the water, curry powder, and the rest of the butter. Bring to a simmer over medium heat. Once at a simmer, reduce the heat and cook gently for 7 minutes, until the fish is fully cooked.

■ Add the tomatoes, hard-boiled eggs, and salt, then remove from the heat. Top with the parsley and serve over cauliflower rice.

SAUTÉED CHICKEN LIVERS
with baby kale salad

■ Yield: 1 serving   ■ Preparation time: 2 minutes   ■ Cook time: 10 minutes

INGREDIENTS

2 tablespoons unsalted butter

4 ounces (115 g) chicken livers, cleaned

Salt and pepper

SALAD:

4 ounces (115 g) baby kale leaves, washed and well drained

2 tablespoons avocado oil

Pinch of salt

INSTRUCTIONS

■ Melt the butter in a large frying pan over medium heat, then add the chicken livers and sear for about 5 minutes before turning them over. Sauté until nicely browned on all sides, about 10 minutes total. If the liver pieces are very thick, they may take a couple of extra minutes to cook. Slice the cooked chicken livers, then season them with a pinch each of salt and pepper.

■ While the livers are cooking, make the salad: Chop the kale and put it in a bowl, then add the avocado oil and salt and toss to coat the kale. Serve the salad topped with the livers for a highly nutritious and delicious meal.

STEAK
WITH ASPARAGUS AND BROCCOLI MASH

This is a simple dinner consisting of protein and vegetables. Add some extra fat in the form of herb butter (see page 168) or avocado oil if you like. My favorite steak for this recipe is a tasty sirloin or tender filet. This method of cooking steak is superior to using the oven or grill, and it tastes great with any keto-approved side.

■ Yield: 1 serving   ■ Preparation time: 5 minutes (not including time to make mash)   ■ Cook time: 8 to 15 minutes

INGREDIENTS

1 (8-ounce/225-g) boneless steak of choice, about 1 inch (2.5 cm) thick

1 tablespoon high-heat cooking oil of choice

5 asparagus spears

1 tablespoon unsalted butter

¼ batch Broccoli Mash (page 192), for serving

FOR A 1-INCH [2.5-CM]-THICK FILET

Blue	1½ mins per side
Rare	2 mins per side
Medium-rare	3 mins per side
Medium	3½ mins per side
Well-done	5 mins per side

INSTRUCTIONS

■ Preheat a heavy-bottomed frying pan over medium-high heat. Oil the steak on both sides before you put it in the pan, and make sure that the pan is hot before you add the steak. Drizzle some oil into the pan; if it separates, it's hot enough.

■ Add the steak to the pan and cook to your desired doneness: blue, rare, medium-rare, medium, or well-done. Blue means it's warm and almost purple inside with very little resistance, and well-done means that it's evenly browned inside with more resistance. Rare, medium-rare, and medium are color variations from red to light pink. Feel the steak with your finger; when it's rare, it's soft. (See the chart at left for more guidance.)

■ After the steak is done, turn off the heat and leave it in the pan for 5 minutes before serving so that it can soak up some extra fat, making it juicier. While the steak is resting, fry the asparagus in a tablespoon of butter over medium-high heat, until softened. Serve the steak with broccoli mash and asparagus.

VARIATION: STEAK WITH MASHED PURPLE CABBAGE.

■ Replace the broccoli mash with cabbage mash (page 195) made from red cabbage.

tips

A steak generally tastes better if you fry it rather than grill it, and you need a thick-bottomed frying pan to do the job. If the steak is too big for your pan, cut it rather than squeeze it in!

The best oil for steak is groundnut oil, which tolerates high temperatures well and doesn't have a strong flavor. Lard also works. Do not use butter.

Make sure that your pan is hot before you place the steak in it. You won't save any time by putting food in a cool pan!

SIDES AND CONDIMENTS

These sides and condiments are great with almost any ketogenic meal. Sometimes people feel that eating keto is restrictive or too repetitive. That is certainly not the case when you use delicious options like these and switch them up for variety!

GUACAMOLE

■ Yield: 1½ cups (350 ml)   ■ Preparation time: 3 minutes

INGREDIENTS

2 ripe avocados

Juice of ½ lime

½ tomato, finely chopped

Pinch of salt

Pinch of cayenne pepper

note ———————

Tomatoes and cayenne pepper can be irritating to sensitive stomachs; for a milder guacamole, omit these ingredients.

INSTRUCTIONS

■ Peel and pit the avocados. Scrape the avocado flesh into a bowl and add the lime juice. Mash with a fork to your desired consistency. Add the tomato and stir to combine. If you want your guacamole really smooth, use a food processor or blender instead. Stir in the salt and cayenne pepper before serving.

VARIATION

■ Add ½ small red onion, finely chopped, to change up the taste and texture.

PESTO

■Yield: 1½ cups (350 ml)   ■Preparation time: 5 minutes

INGREDIENTS

2 ripe avocados

1 tablespoon dried basil

2 cloves garlic

¼ cup (60 ml) pine nuts

2 tablespoons lemon juice

Salt and pepper to taste

2 tablespoons coconut oil, melted

INSTRUCTIONS

■ Peel and pit the avocados. Scrape the flesh into a blender and add the rest of the ingredients, except the coconut oil. Blend until smooth.

■ With the blender running, add the oil in a slow, steady stream until the pesto is creamy.

■ Serve immediately or store in a jar in the refrigerator for up to a week.

note ────────────

Omit the pine nuts if you are sensitive to nuts or follow an autoimmune protocol.

DIFFERENT TYPES *of mash*

The taste and texture of mash goes well with a wide variety of dishes. Here in Scandinavia and throughout northern Europe, potato mash and turnip mash are popular, but you don't need potatoes or other starchy root vegetables to make a great mash. Cabbage and cruciferous vegetables that are free from starch work just as well. They are also a lot healthier for you, as they have a higher nutritional value. Butter is included in these recipes but can be omitted; the result with just the coconut cream will be quite similar.

BROCCOLI MASH

■ Yield: 4 servings   ■ Preparation time: 5 minutes   ■ Cook time: 20 minutes

INGREDIENTS

1 head broccoli

2 scant tablespoons unsalted butter (optional)

½ cup (120 ml) coconut cream

Salt and pepper

note

Broccoli stems are high in fiber. If you suffer from IBS or have a very sensitive stomach, this fiber can cause bloating.

INSTRUCTIONS

■ Cut the broccoli into florets (chop the stem and use it as well, if you like). Put the broccoli in a large saucepan with water. Bring to a simmer and cook for 20 minutes, until the broccoli is tender.

■ Drain the water and transfer the broccoli to a food processor or blender. Add the butter (if using) and coconut cream and blend on high until smooth and creamy. Season with salt and pepper and serve.

CAULIFLOWER MASH

■Yield: 4 servings   ■Preparation time: 5 minutes   ■Cook time: 15 minutes

INGREDIENTS

1 head cauliflower

2 scant tablespoons unsalted butter (optional)

½ cup (120 ml) coconut cream

Salt and pepper

INSTRUCTIONS

■ Cut the cauliflower into florets. Put the florets in a large saucepan with water. Bring to a simmer and cook for 15 minutes, until the cauliflower is tender.

■ Drain the water and transfer the cauliflower to a food processor or blender. Add the butter (if using) and coconut cream and blend on high until smooth and creamy. Season with salt and pepper and serve.

VARIATION

■ Use purple cauliflower instead of regular white cauliflower for a more colorful presentation, as shown on page 149.

CABBAGE MASH

■Yield: 4 servings　■Preparation time: 2 to 3 minutes　■Cook time: 20 minutes

INGREDIENTS

1 head green cabbage

2 scant tablespoons unsalted butter (optional)

½ cup (120 ml) coconut cream

Salt and pepper

INSTRUCTIONS

■ Cut the cabbage into large pieces. Bring a pot of water to a boil, add the cabbage pieces, and boil for 20 minutes, until the cabbage is soft.

■ Drain the water and transfer the cabbage to a food processor or blender. Add the butter (if using) and coconut cream and blend on high until smooth. Season with salt and pepper and serve.

VARIATION

■ Use red cabbage instead of regular green cabbage; it adds an interesting color to this dish!

EGGPLANT MASH

This savory side is best enjoyed with meat rather than fish.

■ Yield: 4 servings ■ Preparation time: 15 minutes ■ Cook time: 5 minutes

INGREDIENTS

1 large eggplant (about 1 pound/455 g)

2 tablespoons unsalted butter, divided

½ cup (120 ml) high-fat, low-sugar yogurt, homemade (page 136) or store-bought

2 cloves garlic

½ teaspoon ground cumin

Salt and pepper

INSTRUCTIONS

■ Peel the eggplant, cut the eggplant into pieces, and remove the seeds. Place the eggplant in a frying pan along with 1 tablespoon of the butter. Fry, stirring, for 5 minutes or until the eggplant is soft.

■ Transfer the eggplant to a blender or food processor and add the yogurt, garlic, cumin, and remaining tablespoon of butter. Blend for 1 minute, then pulse for another 30 seconds. Stop to scrape the sides of the jar if needed, then blend and pulse until smooth. Season with salt and pepper and serve.

taste tip ————————

Add ½ medium red or yellow onion to the mash to vary the flavor. Chop the onion and fry it along with the eggplant before blending.

CAULIFLOWER RICE

This is as close as you can get to eating rice on a keto diet. Cauliflower rice is a great side with fish as well as meat dishes.

■ Yield: 4 servings   ■ Preparation time: 15 minutes   ■ Cook time: 5 minutes

INGREDIENTS

1 head cauliflower

2 tablespoons unsalted butter or coconut cream

2 cloves garlic, minced (optional)

Juice of ½ lime (optional)

1 teaspoon dried cilantro (optional)

INSTRUCTIONS

■ Grate the cauliflower on a box grater until it looks like rice or couscous. If you have a food processor, that works as well.

■ Transfer the cauliflower rice to a frying pan, add the butter and garlic, if using, and fry over medium heat for 5 minutes, stirring as it cooks.

■ Toss with the lime juice and cilantro, if using, and serve.

RADISH FRIES

The type of radish used in this recipe is a winter radish. Winter radishes are white and are about 7 to 8 inches (20 cm) long and 2 inches (5 cm) thick. Radishes contain about 4 percent carbs and are high in fat when fried, which makes these fries a great keto-friendly side dish.

■ Yield: 4 servings   ■ Preparation time: 7 minutes   ■ Cook time: 10 minutes per batch

INGREDIENTS

2 large winter radishes

1 cup (240 ml) coconut oil

Salt

note ───────

Just like regular potato fries, these fries will turn soft and mushy if not eaten right away.

INSTRUCTIONS

■ Peel and cut each radish into sticks that are 3 inches (7.5 cm) long and ½ inch (about 1 cm) thick. Bring a pot of water to a boil, add the radish sticks, and boil for 5 minutes. Drain well, then pat the radishes with a clean kitchen towel to remove the excess water.

■ Heat the oil in a sauté pan over medium-high heat until it is quite hot; you should have about ¾ inch of oil in the pan, enough to submerge the fries. (If needed, add more oil.) To test the temperature, dip the handle of a wooden spoon or chopstick into the oil; if the oil starts bubbling steadily, it is hot enough. Transfer the radish fries to the pan and fry until golden, about 10 minutes, frying them in batches to avoid overcrowding. Season with salt and serve immediately!

PUMPKIN WEDGES

These pumpkin wedges are a nice alternative to potato wedges.

■Yield: 4 servings   ■Preparation time: 5 minutes   ■Cook time: 25 minutes

INGREDIENTS

1 pumpkin (about 8 inches/20 cm across)

2 tablespoons coconut oil, melted

Pinch of salt

INSTRUCTIONS

■ Preheat the oven to 375°F (190°C) and line a rimmed baking sheet with aluminum foil.

■ Peel the pumpkin, cut it in half, and remove the seeds. Cut the pumpkin into wedges and toss them in the coconut oil. Lay the wedges on their sides on the lined baking sheet, spaced ½ inch (about 1 cm) apart. Bake for 25 minutes or until tender. Sprinkle with the salt and serve warm!

COLESLAW

Commercial coleslaw contains sugar: either real sugar or sugar substitutes if it's a low-carb variety. I really don't like the idea of adding sweetness to a meal, even as a flavor enhancer. This keto-approved recipe is a delicious side to pulled pork!

■ Yield: 6 servings ■ Preparation time: 10 minutes (not including time to make mayo)

INGREDIENTS

1½ pounds (700 g) green cabbage

5¼ ounces (150 g) red cabbage

½ yellow onion

¾ cup (180 ml) mayonnaise (page 216)

¼ cup (60 ml) sour cream

2 tablespoons white vinegar

Salt and pepper

INSTRUCTIONS

■ Thinly slice the cabbage and place the slices in a large bowl. Chop the onion and put it in the bowl with the cabbage. Add the mayonnaise and sour cream and stir to combine. Add the vinegar, season with salt and pepper, and toss.

■ Coleslaw tastes better after a few hours in the refrigerator or even the next day, but it can be eaten right away. It will keep in the fridge for up to 5 days.

MARINATED VEGETABLES

This is a nice way of serving vegetables. You can vary the recipe as you like by adding herbs and other flavoring ingredients, and scale it up or down to fit your needs.

■ Yield: One 32-ounce (1-L) jar ■ Preparation time: 10 minutes, plus 30 minutes to marinate
■ Cook time: 15 minutes

INGREDIENTS

BASE SUGGESTIONS (USE ABOUT 4 CUPS/1 L TOTAL):

Bell peppers, cut into ½-inch (1.25-cm) pieces

Broccoli florets

Carrots, cut into sticks

Cauliflower florets

Eggplant, cut into ½-inch (1.25-cm) pieces

Tomatoes, sliced

Yellow onion, chopped

Zucchini, sliced into rounds

FOR THE JAR:

Olive oil

2 cloves garlic, finely chopped

Pinch of salt

INSTRUCTIONS

■ Preheat the oven to 350°F (175°C).

■ Spread the vegetables on a rimmed baking sheet, toss them in some olive oil, and roast for 15 minutes. Remove from the oven and let cool. Transfer the vegetables to a jar and add olive oil, garlic, and a pinch of salt. Place in the refrigerator to marinate for at least 30 minutes.

■ If you completely cover the vegetables in oil, they will keep in the fridge for 1 to 2 weeks; otherwise, consume them within 3 days.

taste tip

You can add fresh herbs, chopped chiles, citrus peels, and feta cheese to the jar as well to vary the flavor.

GHEE

Ghee is an Indian and Pakistani fat that is traditionally made from the milk of holy cows, thus is said to be sacred. Healing properties have been attributed to ghee, probably because it's a pure fat that's been stripped of all its milk proteins. Don't worry if you can't find any holy cows! Just buy grass-fed butter, which has all the nutrients needed to make a healthy and flavorful fat for cooking or adding to meat or vegetables. Unlike butter, you can use ghee for high-heat cooking.

■ Yield: 2 cups (480 ml) ■ Preparation time: 2 minutes ■ Cook time: 20 minutes
■ Special equipment: Fine-mesh strainer or cheesecloth

INGREDIENTS

1 pound (455 g) grass-fed unsalted butter

note ——————

Ghee has a completely different taste than regular butter, and you don't need to use as much of it for cooking.

serving tip ——————

Use on pumpkin wedges (page 202) or steamed vegetables.

INSTRUCTIONS

■ Melt the butter in a saucepan over medium heat; as it simmers, it will slowly separate into three layers. Foam will start to form on the top, while the milk solids and proteins sink to the bottom. Simmer for 15 minutes, until the butter is bright gold in color and the milk protein pieces at the bottom of the pan turn brown. Take the pan off the heat, let cool for 2 minutes, and pour the butter through a fine-mesh or cheesecloth strainer to strain out the solids.

■ Sometimes you need to repeat the straining process; repeat until the ghee is completely clear. It will keep in the refrigerator for up to a month.

Dairy-free
LOW-CARB CHIPS

■ Yield: Sixty 2-inch (5-cm) chips　■ Preparation time: 10 minutes　■ Cook time: 15 minutes

INGREDIENTS

1 large egg white

¾ cup plus 1½ tablespoons (200 ml) almond flour

1 teaspoon chipotle paste

Pinch of salt

serving tip ———
Serve the chips in a pile with melted cheese on top (if you tolerate dairy), or dip them in Guacamole (page 188) or Tomato-Olive Spread (page 217).

INSTRUCTIONS

■ Place an oven rack in the center of the oven and preheat the oven to 300°F (150°C).

■ Lay an 18-inch (46-cm) piece of parchment paper on a work surface, then brush some cooking oil on the paper. (Any keto cooking oil will do.)

■ Whisk the egg white with an electric mixer until frothy. Turn the mixer off and add the almond flour, chipotle paste, and salt. Knead the mixture with your fingers until a dough forms. It shouldn't be sticky; if it's too sticky, add more almond flour.

■ Roll out the dough on the parchment paper until it is about ⅛ inch (3 mm) thick. Cut it into 2-inch (5-cm) triangles. Slide the paper with the chips onto a rimmed baking sheet and bake in the center of the oven for 15 minutes. Make sure that the chips are dry and crispy when you take them out! If they aren't, return them to the oven and continue to bake until crispy, checking them every 5 minutes.

■ Store the chips in a closed container; that way, they will keep their crispness for a couple of days.

CHEESE CHIPS

■ Yield: Sixty 2-inch (5-cm) chips   ■ Preparation time: 5 minutes, plus 30 minutes to cool
■ Cook time: 12 minutes

INGREDIENTS

2 cups (480 ml) shredded semi-soft or semi-hard cheese

½ cup (120 ml) grated Parmesan cheese

½ teaspoon chili powder

½ teaspoon ground cumin

Pinch of salt

INSTRUCTIONS

■ Place an oven rack in the center of the oven and preheat the oven to 400°F (200°C).

■ Line a standard-sized baking sheet with parchment paper, then brush some cooking oil on the paper. (Any keto cooking oil will do.)

■ Spread out the shredded cheese evenly on the parchment paper. Sprinkle the grated Parmesan evenly across the top, then sprinkle the chili powder, cumin, and salt over the cheeses.

■ Place the baking sheet in the center of the oven and bake the chips for 10 minutes, watching them the whole time, as they burn easily! Let cool on the pan for a couple of minutes before cutting. You can use a knife or scissors, as the cheese will be more soft than brittle at this point. Cut the cheese into 2-inch (5-cm) shapes—I prefer triangles.

■ Put the chips back on the parchment paper and bake for 2 more minutes, until crispy. Take them out and let them cool for 30 minutes.

■ Serve the chips in a pile with melted cheese on top. Store in a closed container for up to 5 days.

Mayonnaise, béarnaise, and hollandaise are great sauces that are easy to make and suit a wide variety of dishes. Store-bought sauces often contain preservatives and unnatural flavor enhancers, which you can avoid by making your own. If you find a good brand made with all-natural ingredients, though, using that is fine, too!

HOLLANDAISE

This sauce goes well with whitefish, vegetables, and eggs. It is always served hot.

■ Yield: ½ cup (120 ml)　■ Preparation time: 10 minutes

INGREDIENTS

7 tablespoons (100 g) unsalted butter

2 large egg yolks

1 teaspoon Dijon mustard

1 teaspoon lemon juice

INSTRUCTIONS

■ Melt the butter in a small saucepan. Put the egg yolks in a heatproof bowl and set it on top of a saucepan of simmering water. Add the mustard and lemon juice to the bowl with the egg yolks and whisk carefully. Slowly pour the melted butter into the yolk mixture, whisking constantly. Continue whisking until the hollandaise is thick and creamy, 2 to 3 minutes. Use immediately.

■ The hollandaise will keep in a jar in the refrigerator for up to a week.

tip ——————————————

Have an ice cube ready in case the hollandaise starts to separate. Drop the cube into the sauce and whisk it in, and your sauce is saved!

BÉARNAISE

Béarnaise, one of the French "mother sauces," can be enjoyed hot or cold. It goes well with hearty meats, like steak.

■ Yield: 2 cups (480 ml) ■ Preparation time: 15 minutes

INGREDIENTS

2 large egg yolks

¼ cup (60 ml) white wine vinegar

1 tablespoon water

10 tablespoons plus 2 teaspoons (150 g) unsalted butter, softened or melted

Salt

INSTRUCTIONS

■ Put the egg yolks in a metal bowl and whisk with an electric mixer or stick blender. While whisking, add the vinegar and water.

■ Fill a saucepan with water and bring to a simmer. Place the bowl with the yolk mixture on top of the saucepan, without letting the bottom of the bowl touch the water. Whisk the mixture until it thickens, then slowly whisk in the butter. Season with salt and serve immediately or place in the refrigerator to chill before serving.

■ Store the béarnaise in a jar in the refrigerator for up to a week.

VARIATION: CHILI BÉARNAISE.

■ Before beginning the recipe, add 1 small yellow onion, finely chopped, and ½ teaspoon chili powder or cayenne pepper to the white wine vinegar. Boil for 1 minute, let cool, and then proceed with the base recipe.

MAYONNAISE

This cold sauce goes well with practically everything on a ketogenic menu, and it's the base for aioli and remoulade sauce (mayonnaise mixed with herbs, mustard, and capers).

■Yield: 2 cups (480 ml)　■Preparation time: 5 minutes

INGREDIENTS

2 large egg yolks, at room temperature

1½ cups (360 ml) light-tasting olive oil

Juice of ½ lime, at room temperature

Salt and pepper

INSTRUCTIONS

■ Take the eggs and lime out of the refrigerator an hour before beginning the recipe to make sure that they're at room temperature; this helps the ingredients emulsify well when blended together.

■ Put the egg yolks in a bowl and mix with a stick blender until smooth. With the blender running, carefully add the olive oil drop by drop until the mayonnaise starts to thicken. When thick, add the lime juice and salt and pepper to taste, then stir with a fork or mix with the stick blender until combined.

■ Store in a jar in the refrigerator for up to a week.

TOMATO-OLIVE SPREAD

This is a flavorful filler for wraps and works as a side dish for meat as well as fish. You also can use it as a dip for keto-friendly chips (pages 208 and 210), fries (page 200), and chicharrones.

■Yield: ½ cup (120 ml)   ■Preparation time: 5 minutes

INGREDIENTS

4 ounces (115 g) cream cheese, softened

12 pitted green olives

7 sun-dried tomatoes

4 large fresh basil leaves

1 teaspoon tomato puree

Salt and pepper to taste

INSTRUCTIONS

■ Put all the ingredients in a food processor and mix until smooth.

VARIATION

■ Replace the olives with ½ cup (120 ml) grated Parmesan cheese.

TUNA PÂTÉ

Eat this tuna pâté with boiled eggs for breakfast, serve it in a salad wrap, or use it as a spread on Keto Crispbread (page 132).

■Yield: 4 servings ■Preparation time: 5 minutes (not including time to make mayo)

INGREDIENTS

1 (5-ounce/142-g) can tuna packed in water or oil

2 tablespoons mayonnaise (page 216)

1 tablespoon chili sauce (optional)

Salt and pepper to taste

INSTRUCTIONS

■ Drain the water or oil from the tuna. Place all the ingredients in a food processor and mix until smooth.

VARIATION

■ Add fresh herbs, olives, or pesto (page 190) to make the pâté a little more interesting!

DRIED OLIVES

This is an easy and interesting snack (or side) that can be tossed into a salad or chopped and used as a coating for oven-baked fish.

■ Yield: 4 servings   ■ Cook time: 15 minutes

INGREDIENTS

1 (6-ounce/170-g) can pitted green olives (about 1 cup/240 ml)

INSTRUCTIONS

- Drain the olives and place them on a heatproof plate. Microwave on high for 3 to 4 minutes, open the microwave, and shake the plate. Repeat 4 or 5 times until the olives are completely dry.

- Serve immediately while still hot and crunchy.

SNACKS AND DESSERTS

As the ketogenic diet is gaining in popularity, a ton of new recipes are hitting the internet, especially snacks and desserts. I've deliberately chosen to keep this section short, because a keto diet will eventually eliminate most of your desire for sweet-tasting foods. It's nice to have some alternatives once in a while, though, because most of the gluten-free and "sugar-free" options available at cafés and restaurants are far from low-carb.

For a dessert to be ketogenic, it cannot be too sweet, and it needs to contain a fair amount of fat. Otherwise, it might lead to cravings or bingeing instead of preventing them. This section includes two different types of fat bombs, chocolate and coconut balls, ice cream, and panna cotta, which can be varied in a number of ways. After you have made these simple treats a couple of times, you can experiment with other flavoring ingredients, such as berries and nuts, as long as you keep the fat content above 60 percent.

The trick is to use a good fat as a base, such as coconut oil. I discuss this amazing high-quality fat in depth on page 58. If you tolerate dairy, butter is a great choice as well.

FAT *bombs*

I began experimenting with fat bombs many years before Fatty Coffee (page 238) was introduced to me. I was looking for a keto-friendly way to curb cravings and boost ketones before workouts. Pure fat doesn't interfere with your blood sugar and is very satiating, even in the form of a small treat. One or two of these fat bombs are enough for a small snack, so don't go overboard just because they are keto-approved! A snack should never replace a meal, so if you are hungry, opt for a full meal instead.

I typically use fat bombs either as quick fuel before I go to the gym or when I want something sweet to go with my coffee. For any type of training, though, you want to avoid eating a big meal less than two hours beforehand. If you experience hunger before your scheduled training, postpone any larger calorie intake until afterward. Eating before training will impede your performance, so just pop a fat bomb and go!

CHOCOLATY AND MINTY *fat bombs*

Mint is a refreshing flavor to pair with fat. I personally prefer fresh, herbaceous flavors over sweet because sweet tends to leave you wanting more. Peppermint also has a calming effect on the stomach, so these fat bombs can be very beneficial if you suffer from IBS, stomach cramps, or general stomach upset.

■ Yield: 12 fat bombs   ■ Preparation time: 15 minutes, plus 1 to 2 hours to chill
■ Special equipment: Silicone mold with twelve ½-ounce (20-ml) cavities

INGREDIENTS

½ cup (120 ml) coconut oil

¼ cup (60 ml) unsweetened cocoa powder

1 teaspoon vanilla extract

20 drops peppermint oil

10 drops liquid stevia

Pinch of salt (optional)

INSTRUCTIONS

■ Warm the coconut oil in a saucepan just until it liquefies, then pour it into a blender. Add the rest of the ingredients to the blender and blend until smooth. Pour the mixture into the silicone mold and place in the refrigerator until solid, 1 to 2 hours.

■ When solid, pop the fat bombs out of the mold. Store in a jar in the refrigerator, where they will keep for several weeks (if they last that long). Eat them chilled, directly from the fridge, as they will melt at room temperature.

taste tip
The lack of sugar in keto snacks creates a much less sweet treat than you may be used to, but bear in mind that fat bombs taste better after they are set.

SOUR BOMBS

■ Yield: 12 fat bombs ■ Preparation time: 15 minutes, plus 1 to 2 hours to chill
■ Special equipment: Silicone mold with twelve ½-ounce (20-ml) cavities

INGREDIENTS

8 ounces (225 g) coconut butter

3 tablespoons coconut oil

Grated zest of 1 lemon

2 tablespoons lemon juice

10 drops liquid stevia, natural or vanilla-flavored

INSTRUCTIONS

■ Warm the coconut butter and coconut oil in a saucepan just until the mixture liquefies. Pour into a blender, add the lemon zest, lemon juice, and stevia, and blend until smooth. Pour into the silicone mold and place in the refrigerator until solid, 1 to 2 hours.

■ When solid, pop the fat bombs out of the mold. Store in a jar in the refrigerator, where they will keep for several weeks. Enjoy chilled, directly from the fridge, as they will melt at room temperature.

No-bake CHOCOLATE BALLS

Everyone likes chocolate, even those who are not high-fat enthusiasts. These chocolate balls go well with coffee and also work nicely as small after-dinner treats. They are fine to serve to your non-keto friends, who will have a hard time distinguishing them from regular chocolate balls.

The base for this treat is butter and shredded coconut; it's a great high-fat base that can be varied endlessly. I share three of my personal favorites on this and the following pages, but you can browse online for more ideas and inspiration.

■ Yield: 15 balls   ■ Preparation time: 15 minutes, plus 1 to 2 hours to chill

INGREDIENTS

7 tablespoons (100 g) unsalted butter, softened

7 ounces (200 g) unsweetened shredded coconut, plus extra for coating

2 tablespoons unsweetened cocoa powder

2 tablespoons strong brewed coffee (optional)

1 teaspoon ground cinnamon

10 drops liquid stevia

INSTRUCTIONS

■ To make the job of mixing the ingredients easier, take the butter out of the refrigerator an hour before you begin the recipe. Place all the ingredients in a bowl and mix with your fingers until everything is well combined. (You can use a fork for this step if you don't like getting your fingers into gooey things.)

■ Roll the mixture into 1-inch (2.5-cm) balls, toss the balls in shredded coconut, and place in the refrigerator to chill for at least 1 hour. They taste better when cold, so store them in the refrigerator, even though they won't melt at room temperature. The chocolate balls will keep in the refrigerator for weeks.

taste tip

Strong coffee plus cocoa powder gives these chocolate balls a mature taste. If you want to enhance this further, you can add a teaspoon of rum or brandy as well. The coffee and cocoa can be replaced with licorice powder, vanilla extract, or any other flavoring ingredients you want to try. Adjust the amounts as you see fit; you don't have to be exact here. The texture and yield are determined mostly by the amounts of butter and shredded coconut you use.

Nutty CHOCOLATE BALLS

These balls contain nut butter, but it can be omitted if you are sensitive to nuts or just want to change up the recipe. In general, I prefer to use pecan butter or macadamia nut butter, as they are delicious and relatively low in carbohydrates compared to other nut butters. You can use peanut butter or cashew butter as well, but they have higher carb contents along with more of the inflammatory omega-6 fatty acids.

If you buy nut butter from the store, look carefully at the list of ingredients. Some manufacturers add sugar and non-keto vegetable oils; please avoid these products! Learn how to make your own healthy nut butters on page 268.

■ Yield: 15 balls ■ Preparation time: 15 minutes, plus 1 to 2 hours to chill

INGREDIENTS

10 tablespoons plus 2 teaspoons (150 g) unsalted butter, softened

3½ ounces (100 g) unsweetened coconut flakes, toasted if desired

2 tablespoons unsweetened cocoa powder

5 tablespoons pecan butter

15 drops liquid stevia

INSTRUCTIONS

■ To make the job of mixing the ingredients easier, take the butter out of the refrigerator an hour before you begin the recipe. Put all the ingredients in a bowl and mix with your fingers until everything is well combined. (You can use a fork for this step if you don't like getting your fingers into gooey things.)

■ Roll the mixture into 1-inch (2.5-cm) balls and place in the refrigerator to chill for at least 1 hour. They taste better when cold, so keep them in the refrigerator, even though they won't melt at room temperature. The chocolate balls will keep in the refrigerator for weeks.

NUT-FREE SUGGESTIONS

■ You can substitute coconut butter for the pecan butter. Coconut butter and coconut oil are totally different products; the butter is much sweeter. If you go with this alternative, you can omit the stevia. You also can replace the pecan butter with same amount of unsalted dairy butter.

COCONUT BALLS

This is a lovely treat for anyone who loves coconut—a sweet and healthy snack consisting of shredded coconut, coconut butter, and coconut cream!

■ Yield: 12 balls   ■ Preparation time: 15 minutes, plus 1 to 2 hours to chill

INGREDIENTS

7 ounces (200 g) unsweetened shredded coconut, plus extra for coating

3½ ounces (100 g) coconut butter

3 tablespoons coconut cream

1 teaspoon vanilla extract

INSTRUCTIONS

■ Put all the ingredients in a bowl and mix with a fork until well blended. Roll the mixture into 1-inch (2.5-cm) balls; if this is difficult to do, put the bowl in the fridge for 30 minutes, then try again. Coconut butter can get too soft and liquid-y at room temperature.

■ Roll the balls in shredded coconut and place in the refrigerator to chill for at least 1 hour. They will melt at room temperature, so make sure to keep them in the refrigerator, where they will keep for weeks.

Instant RASPBERRY AVOCADO ICE CREAM

This is by far the healthiest ice cream I have ever seen, packed with nutrients and delicious on a hot summer day. The base is avocados and frozen berries, and it's ready right away!

■Yield: 6 servings ■Preparation time: 10 minutes

INGREDIENTS

3 ripe avocados

4 cups (1 L) frozen raspberries

Juice of ½ lime

1 teaspoon vanilla extract

15 drops liquid stevia

INSTRUCTIONS

■ Peel and pit the avocados. Scrape the flesh into a bowl, add the raspberries, and mix with a stick blender until smooth. Squeeze in the lime juice, add the vanilla extract and stevia, and mix with a fork or spatula. Scoop into serving bowls and enjoy right away.

No-churn
KETO
ICE CREAM

Because the eggs in this recipe aren't cooked, it's important that they be pasteurized. Pasteurized eggs can be purchased from the supermarket, or you can pasteurize eggs yourself by following the instructions below.

■ Yield: 6 servings   ■ Preparation time: 20 minutes, plus 2 hours to freeze

INGREDIENTS

4 large pasteurized eggs

½ cup (120 ml) powdered erythritol

1¼ cups (300 ml) coconut cream or heavy cream

1 tablespoon vanilla extract

taste tip

Add berries, roasted pecans, toasted coconut flakes, or any other flavoring ingredient you like—the possibilities are endless!

HOW TO PASTEURIZE EGGS AT HOME

■ Put the eggs in a saucepan and cover with water. Heat the water to 140°F (60°C) and keep the eggs in the water for 3 to 5 minutes at that temperature. Use a thermometer to monitor the temperature of the water; do not allow it to exceed 148°F (64°C).

INSTRUCTIONS

■ Separate the eggs, putting the whites in a medium-sized mixing bowl and the yolks in a smaller bowl. Whisk the whites until stiff peaks form; when you can turn the bowl upside down without the whipped whites falling out, they are sufficiently firm. Slowly add the erythritol, while whisking. In a large mixing bowl, whip the cream until peaks form. Gently fold the whipped egg whites into the whipped cream.

■ Add the vanilla extract to the bowl with the yolks and whisk well to combine. Gently fold the yolk mixture into the whipped egg white and cream mixture and place in the freezer for a minimum of 2 hours.

■ Take the ice cream out of the freezer 30 minutes before serving to make sure it's not too hard. If you want softer ice cream, you can add 2 to 4 tablespoons of MCT oil (see page 58) before freezing.

Dairy-free BLUEBERRY PANNA COTTA

Panna cotta is a perfect dessert if you're having friends over for dinner. It's easy to make, it looks elegant, and it's delicious! It needs to chill for a couple of hours, so I recommend making it the night before. The panna cotta tastes better when it has some time to set.

■ Yield: 6 servings   ■ Preparation time: 15 minutes, plus 6 hours to chill

INGREDIENTS

2 heaping tablespoons gelatin powder

1½ cups (360 ml) coconut cream (or unsalted butter if not dairy-sensitive)

3 tablespoons coconut cream

1 cup (240 ml) water

1 teaspoon vanilla extract

10 drops liquid stevia

TOPPING:

2 heaping teaspoons gelatin powder

1 cup (240 ml) blueberries

taste tip

Panna cotta can be varied endlessly; try lemon or lime juice, unsweetened cocoa powder, nuts and nut butters, or all kinds of berries!

INSTRUCTIONS

■ Put the gelatin powder in a small glass and add boiling water to cover by 1 inch. Stir well for 30 seconds, then let it sit for 10 minutes.

■ Place the coconut cream, coconut cream, and water in a saucepan and heat, while stirring, but do not let it boil. Add the gelatin, still stirring, then add the vanilla extract and stevia.

■ Pour the mixture into six 6-ounce (200-ml) serving bowls and place in the refrigerator until set, about 4 hours. Don't add the topping until the base is set; you can do this the next day, as the topping needs less time to set.

■ To make the topping, pour the gelatin into a small glass, add boiling water to cover by 1 inch, stir well for 30 seconds, then let it sit for 10 minutes.

■ Mix the blueberries with a stick blender until smooth. Put them in a small saucepan and heat, but do not allow them to boil. Stir in the gelatin for a minute, then take the pan off the heat. Take the serving glasses or bowls with the base out of the refrigerator and carefully add some of the blueberry topping to each bowl. Put the bowls back in the refrigerator and chill for at least 2 more hours.

DRINKS AND SMOOTHIES

Drinks and smoothies are an easy way to get in extra fats, proteins, and other nutrients. They are great for people on the go because they are quick to prepare and very portable. You can even enjoy one of the protein shakes in this section as a substitute for a meal. Smoothies can be nutritious, detoxifying, and delicious, and the teas I'm sharing have healing properties. All the recipes in this section are perfect tools for speeding up keto-adaptation.

FATTY COFFEE

Fatty Coffee was originally yak butter tea. It was brought to the United States by famed biohacker Dave Asprey, who encountered this ancient traditional drink in Tibet. Many low-carb enthusiasts have been using it ever since. Bear in mind that coffee usually contains a small amount of microtoxins and that the stimulating effects of caffeine might interfere with healing and keto-adaptation. However, as a coffee drinker myself, I do love my Fatty Coffee!

■ Yield: 1 serving   ■ Preparation time: 1 minute (not including time to brew coffee)

INGREDIENTS

1 cup (240 ml) hot brewed coffee

1½ tablespoons unsalted butter

1½ teaspoons coconut oil or MCT oil (see page 58)

INSTRUCTIONS

■ Pour the coffee into a blender. Add the butter and oil and blend on high until smooth and frothy, about 30 seconds. Serve hot.

keto tip

Add an egg yolk to increase the nutritional value. It won't affect the taste very much, but it will add a whole lot of vitamins and minerals to the drink!

BLOOD SUGAR TEA

As an alternative to Fatty Coffee (page 238), you can make this blood sugar–lowering tea. The main ingredient is Ceylon cinnamon, but cassia, ginger, cloves, and sage are known for possessing similar properties. Tea made from herbs, spices, flowers, and leaves is a great alternative to regular tea (see "How to Make Your Own Teas" on page 272 for details).

■Yield: 1 serving (1 cup/240 ml)   ■Preparation time: 6 minutes

INGREDIENTS

¾ teaspoon ground Ceylon cinnamon

1 cup (240 ml) hot water

1 tablespoon coconut milk or heavy cream

1 tablespoon coconut oil or MCT oil (see page 58)

3 drops liquid stevia (optional)

INSTRUCTIONS

■ Fill a tea strainer with the cinnamon and put it in a cup with the hot water (175°F/80°C). Let it steep for 5 minutes, remove the strainer, and pour the tea into a blender. Add the coconut milk, oil, and stevia, if using, and blend on high for 30 seconds. Pour it back into the cup and enjoy your drink!

TURMERIC GOLDEN TEA

This lovely tea is like liquid gold—it aids digestion, boosts immune function, and supports liver health. It's an excellent evening drink as well as a detox aid that has been around in traditional Indian medicine for thousands of years.

This recipe contains black pepper and cayenne pepper, which are traditionally used to increase the absorption of micronutrients.

■ Yield: 1 serving (1 cup/240 ml)   ■ Preparation time: 5 minutes

INGREDIENTS

1 cup (240 ml) coconut milk

1 teaspoon turmeric powder

¼ teaspoon ginger powder

Pinch of ground black pepper (optional)

Pinch of cayenne pepper (optional)

INSTRUCTIONS

■ Place the ingredients in a small saucepan and heat until hot but not boiling. Stir, remove from the heat, and let cool for a minute before drinking.

tip ───────────────
You can make a bigger batch of this tea and store it in the refrigerator; it will keep for days and taste just as good when reheated.

EGG MILK

Egg milk tastes almost exactly like dairy milk; it's a great dairy-free milk substitute! You can use it for cooking, add it to tea or coffee, or drink it as is.

■ Yield: 1 quart (1 L) ■ Preparation time: 5 minutes

INGREDIENTS

1 quart (1 L) boiling water

4 tablespoons (55 g) unsalted butter

2 large egg yolks

note ———

You can use whole eggs if you want to, but the milk will need to be blended longer (about 1 minute), and if you let it cool, it will need to be gently reheated, otherwise the whites will clump together. Don't throw it out if you see some clumps after it cools; just blend it again for a minute or two to make it nice and smooth.

INSTRUCTIONS

■ Pour the boiling water into a blender, add the butter and egg yolks, and blend on high until smooth and frothy. Drink right away, try some of the variations below, or store in the refrigerator for up to 2 days. Reheat before serving.

VARIATION: CHOCOLATE EGG MILK.

■ Add 1 tablespoon unsweetened cocoa powder and sweeten with 15 drops liquid stevia.

VARIATION: CINNAMON EGG MILK.

■ Add 1 teaspoon ground cinnamon and sweeten with 15 drops liquid stevia.

VARIATION: CAFÉ LATTE.

■ Add $1/3$ cup (80 ml) strong brewed coffee to $1/2$ cup (120 ml) of egg milk.

I'm a smoothie lover and drink smoothies primarily for two reasons: to up my fat intake and to up my intake of chlorophylls, which contain important micronutrients and antioxidants! A lot of super-healthy foods like algae aren't very tasty, but they can be quite palatable when prepared properly!

One of the simplest, most everyday ingredients has a huge impact: ice! I think a few ice cubes make smoothies much better, especially green smoothies.

IMMUNE BOOSTER
smoothie

■ Yield: 1 serving (1 cup/240 ml)   ■ Preparation time: 3 minutes

INGREDIENTS

1 ripe avocado

1 cup (240 ml) water

$1/3$ cup (80 ml) frozen broccoli

1 tablespoon MCT oil (see page 58)

1 teaspoon chlorella powder

1 teaspoon ginger powder

1 teaspoon spirulina powder

2 large fresh mint leaves

A couple of ice cubes

INSTRUCTIONS

■ Peel and pit the avocado and put the avocado flesh in a blender. Add the rest of the ingredients and blend on high until smooth and frothy. Pour into a glass and enjoy immediately!

VARIATION: IMMUNO SHOT.

■ In a blender, combine $1/3$ cup (80 ml) water, 1 teaspoon chlorella powder, 1 teaspoon spirulina powder, 10 drops lemon juice concentrate, and $1/2$ teaspoon ginger powder. Blend on high for 20 seconds or until smooth. Enjoy immediately.

KETONE BOOSTER
smoothie

■ Yield: 1 serving (2 cups/480 ml)   ■ Preparation time: 3 minutes

INGREDIENTS

½ cup (120 ml) ice

½ cup (120 ml) coconut cream

¹/₃ cup (80 ml) blueberries (optional)

1 tablespoon coconut oil

1 tablespoon MCT oil (see page 58)

10 drops liquid stevia

INSTRUCTIONS

■ Put all the ingredients in a blender and blend on high until smooth and frothy. Pour into a big glass and enjoy immediately!

NATURAL *protein shakes*

There are a lot of protein powders out there, and if you do a lot of gym training, you have probably tried a few of them already. Protein powders are generally made from highly insulinemic milk proteins that spike insulin and inhibit ketone production. If you want your protein shakes to be keto-friendly, you need to add some fat. I suggest leaving the protein powders behind and instead using whole eggs, which provide the necessary protein and fat.

These two protein shakes are satiating and nutritious and have a large quantity of good proteins with high bioavailability.

SWEET CINNAMON
protein shake

■ Yield: 1 serving (2 cups/480 ml)   ■ Preparation time: 3 minutes

INGREDIENTS

1 cup (240 ml) water

1 cup (240 ml) coconut milk or unsweetened almond milk

1/3 cup (60 ml) ice

2 large pasteurized eggs (see page 232)

1½ teaspoons ground cinnamon

5 drops liquid stevia (optional)

INSTRUCTIONS

■ Put all the ingredients in a blender and blend on high until smooth and frothy. Pour into a big glass and enjoy immediately!

keto tip

This smoothie is a great meal replacement if you are in a hurry or need an efficient post-workout drink.

GREEN
protein shake

■ Yield: 1 serving (2 cups/480 ml) ■ Preparation time: 3 minutes

INGREDIENTS

2 cups (480 ml) water or
unsweetened almond milk

$^1/_3$ cup (60 ml) ice

2 large pasteurized eggs
(see page 232)

1 ripe avocado, peeled and
pitted

1 tablespoon MCT oil
(see page 58)

INSTRUCTIONS

■ Put all the ingredients in a blender and blend on high until smooth.
Enjoy immediately.

keto tip ───────────────

*This smoothie is a great meal replacement if you
are in a hurry or need an efficient post-workout
drink.*

CREAMY CINNAMON
keto smoothie

■ Yield: 1 serving (2 cups/480 ml)　■ Preparation time: 3 minutes

INGREDIENTS

2 cups (480 ml)
unsweetened almond milk
or coconut milk

$1/3$ cup (60 ml) ice

1 teaspoon ground
cinnamon

1 teaspoon guar gum

15 drops liquid stevia

INSTRUCTIONS

■ Put all the ingredients in a blender and blend on high until smooth
and frothy; the guar gum will thicken the smoothie in just a few
seconds. Pour into a big glass and enjoy immediately!

VARIATION

■ This smoothie can also be enjoyed as a hot drink; omit the ice and
microwave it or heat it up in a small saucepan on the stove.

BLACKBERRY CHEESECAKE
keto smoothie

■ Yield: 1 serving (2 cups/480 ml)   ■ Preparation time: 3 minutes

INGREDIENTS

½ cup (120 ml) water

½ cup (60 g) frozen blackberries

¼ cup (60 ml) heavy cream or coconut cream (see page 264)

2 ounces (55 g) cream cheese or whipped coconut cream

1 tablespoon MCT oil (see page 58)

½ teaspoon vanilla extract

10 drops liquid stevia (optional)

INSTRUCTIONS

■ Put all the ingredients in a blender and blend on high until smooth. Enjoy immediately.

VARIATION

■ Swap out the blackberries for whatever other berries are in season; this smoothie tastes great with raspberries and blueberries as well. Avoid all other fruits except avocado.

PUMPKIN
latte

Pumpkin is not super keto; the carbohydrate content is around 6 percent, but you can get away with it as long as you combine it with high-fat ingredients.

The base of this smoothie is pumpkin puree. You can buy organic pumpkin puree in any natural foods store or make your own. You just need a pie pumpkin and a stick blender: Cut the pumpkin in half, scoop out the seeds, then roast it, cut side down, at 350°F (175°C), until the flesh is easily pierced with a knife. Remove the pumpkin from the oven, scoop out the flesh, and blend it until smooth with the stick blender.

■Yield: 1 serving (2 cups/480 ml)   ■Preparation time: 3 minutes

INGREDIENTS

1 cup (240 ml) unsweetened almond milk

½ cup (120 ml) heavy cream or coconut cream

2 ounces (55 g) pumpkin puree

1 tablespoon MCT oil (see page 58)

½ teaspoon pumpkin pie spice

10 drops liquid stevia

INSTRUCTIONS

■ Put all the ingredients in a blender and blend on high until smooth. Pour the mixture into a small saucepan and heat it up on the stove, making sure it doesn't boil. Serve hot.

VARIATION

■ To make a pumpkin smoothie, add some ice cubes to the blender and serve the drink cold.

PECAN BUTTER
smoothie

■ Yield: 1 serving (2 cups/480 ml)   ■ Preparation time: 3 minutes

INGREDIENTS

1 cup (240 ml) coconut milk

1 tablespoon unsweetened cocoa powder

2 heaping tablespoons pecan butter

5 drops liquid stevia

INSTRUCTIONS

■ Put all the ingredients in a blender and blend on high until smooth. Enjoy immediately.

VARIATION

■ This smoothie can also be enjoyed as a hot drink. Just put it in a small saucepan and heat it up on the stove, making sure it doesn't boil.

HOW TO...

This how-to section shows you how to make some popular keto staples yourself. Almost all of these staples are available at your local natural foods store, but if you like to do things yourself, these recipes are for you. They are really simple! Here, you will learn how to turn coconut milk into coconut cream; how to make delicious nut butters, milks, and flours; and how to make your own teas!

How to MAKE COCONUT CREAM

Coconut cream is like coconut milk but with a higher fat percentage, generally around 20 percent. Coconut cream can be purchased in cans, which saves you the step of making it yourself. Be careful, though, to avoid a product called "cream of coconut," which contains sugar and other additives and is used principally to make cocktails. You can also "make" your own coconut cream using full-fat coconut milk, following the method below.

- Yield: 1¼ cups (300 ml) per 15-ounce (450-ml) can
- Preparation time: 15 minutes, plus time to chill the can of coconut milk overnight

INGREDIENTS

1 (15-ounce/450-ml) can full-fat coconut milk

INSTRUCTIONS

- Refrigerate the can of coconut milk overnight; this will make the milk separate into liquid and solid parts. Open the can and scoop off just the solid part that has risen to the top (this is the cream). Use the coconut water for smoothies. Store the cream in the refrigerator and use within a week.

How to MAKE WHIPPED COCONUT CREAM

It can be tricky to make a low-carb dairy-free whipped cream that has the same texture as whipped dairy cream. This is the method I use.

- Yield: 1¼ cups (300 ml)   - Preparation time: 15 minutes

INGREDIENTS

1¾ cups (420 ml) coconut cream

Powdered erythritol (up to ⅓ cup/80 ml per can of coconut cream) (optional)

1 teaspoon vanilla extract (optional)

INSTRUCTIONS

- Beat the coconut cream with an electric mixer until creamy and fluffy. It will take 10 to 15 minutes. Stir in the vanilla.

How to
MAKE COCONUT BUTTER

Buy unsweetened shredded coconut or coconut flakes. A whole coconut works, too, but it requires some effort to open it and carve out the coconut meat. However, if you're into DIY stuff, it can be a lot of fun!

You can roast the coconut in the oven before processing; most commercial coconut butters are made with roasted coconut. This loosens the oils and makes a creamier butter. To roast shredded coconut or coconut flakes, preheat the oven to 350°F (175°C). Put the coconut on a rimmed baking sheet and roast for 5 to 10 minutes, until slightly golden. The coconut will be light brown when it's done.

■Yield: 8 ounces (225 g)   ■Preparation time: 20 minutes
■Special equipment: Food processor or high-speed blender

INGREDIENTS

8 ounces (225 g) unsweetened shredded coconut or coconut flakes

INSTRUCTIONS

■ Put the coconut in a food processor or high-speed blender and blend on high, stopping and scraping down the sides as needed. The coconut will start to pull together into butter after 10 to 15 minutes, so keep blending until you are satisfied with the texture. Blend for 20 minutes if you want it super-smooth. Store it in a container in the refrigerator, where it will keep for weeks.

How to MAKE YOUR OWN FLOUR

Making your own flour out of, for example, almonds or coconut is a simple process; you just need a food processor or high-speed blender with a pulse function.

This recipe is for almond flour, but you can repeat the process with any nuts or unsweetened shredded coconut.

- Yield: 3½ ounces (100 g) ■ Preparation time: 20 seconds
- Special equipment: Food processor or high-speed blender

INGREDIENTS

5 ounces (140 g) whole raw almonds

tip

You can use blanched slivered almonds instead of whole almonds; slivered almonds are generally cheaper. Because the almond skins are removed, you will end up with a finer-textured flour.

INSTRUCTIONS

- Put the almonds in a food processor or high-speed blender and pulse for about 20 seconds; they will turn powdery pretty fast. If you pulse too long, the almonds will begin to clump together and eventually turn into butter.

How to MAKE PEANUT BUTTER AND NUT BUTTERS

Nut butters are made according to the same basic protocol as coconut butter (see page 265), except that for those nuts that are less fatty, you might want to add oil or dairy butter. It's also a question of personal taste—how sticky, crunchy, or smooth you want your nut butter to be.

You can use this same basic recipe to make peanut butter or any type of nut butter. You can make nut butter out of almonds, macadamia nuts, cashews, and pecans, to name just a few of the possibilities. The only difference is that the oil or butter, if added, should complement the flavor of the nut or be neutral.

■ Yield: 1½ cups (360 ml)   ■ Preparation time: 10 minutes
■ Special equipment: Food processor or high-speed blender

INGREDIENTS

2 cups (480 ml) raw or roasted unsalted peanuts or nuts of choice

1 to 2 tablespoons oil, if needed (see suggestions below)

½ teaspoon salt

tip

You can roast the peanuts or nuts in the oven before processing; most commercial peanut and nut butters are made with roasted nuts. This loosens the oils and makes a creamier butter. To roast nuts, preheat the oven to 350°F (175°C). Put the nuts on a rimmed baking sheet and roast for 10 to 15 minutes, until slightly golden and aromatic.

INSTRUCTIONS

■ Put the peanuts or nuts in a food processor or high-speed blender and process on high for 5 minutes, regularly stopping and scraping down the sides. The peanuts or nuts will go through various stages: first they will look like couscous, but the more you blend, the more oils they will release. If the butter is still too dry, add the oil and salt to taste. Blend until you're satisfied with the texture.

■ Transfer the nut butter to a jar and store in the refrigerator; it will keep for several weeks.

SUGGESTED OILS FOR BUTTERS

■ If making peanut butter, use peanut oil, if needed; if making a nut butter, use refined coconut oil, MCT oil, or dairy butter if the nut butter needs extra creaminess. Never use olive oil, which has too strong a flavor.

VARIATION

■ To make a chunky peanut or nut butter, reserve 1.7 ounces (50 g) of peanuts or nuts and chop them separately. Add them to the butter in the last stage of the blending process and stir with a fork or spoon to combine until you are satisfied with the texture.

How to
MAKE COCONUT MILK AND NUT MILK

This recipe is for coconut milk or almond milk, but you can use the same method to make other types of nut milk, such as cashew or macadamia.

■ Yield: 2 cups (480 ml) ■ Preparation time: 15 minutes, plus at least 8 hours to soak
■ Special equipment: Fine-mesh strainer or cheesecloth

INGREDIENTS

1 cup (240 ml) unsweetened shredded coconut or raw almonds

2 cups (480 ml) water, plus extra for soaking

5 drops liquid stevia (optional)

tip

Use coconut milk or almond milk for baking, in smoothies, or as a dairy milk substitute in your morning coffee.

INSTRUCTIONS

■ Place the coconut or almonds in a bowl and cover with water. Make sure that they are covered by about 1 inch (2.5 cm) of water so that there's room for swelling. Cover the bowl with a cloth and leave on the counter overnight, or for a minimum of 8 hours.

■ Drain the soaking water. If using almonds, rinse the almonds thoroughly under running water. (The soaking water contains inflammatory phytic acid, and you don't want that in your almond milk.)

■ Put the coconut or rinsed almonds in a blender, add the 2 cups (480 ml) of fresh water, and blend on high for 2 to 4 minutes, alternating between blending and pulsing.

■ Place a fine-mesh strainer or colander lined with clean cheesecloth over a container, then pour the coconut or almond mixture through it. If using a fine-mesh strainer, press against the nut pulp with a large spoon or rubber spatula to extract all the milk; if using a cheesecloth, gather up the sides of the cloth to form a bundle and squeeze firmly with clean hands to extract all of the milk. When you have about 2 cups (480 ml) of milk, you can add the sweetener, if using.

■ Store the milk in the refrigerator for up to 3 days.

How to
MAKE YOUR OWN TEAS

The study of herbs, plants, leaves, and flowers can be very enlightening, especially as you learn about their incredible medicinal properties (see below for a list of my favorites). Best of all, you don't need to buy teabags or loose herbal teas from the store. You can make your own teas from your own garden or indoor plants! Drying your own herbs is economically savvy because prices can be quite high at the grocery store. If you dry your own herbs, they will also be fresher and more potent. Dried herbs remain potent for about a year, but the ones in the grocery store might be a lot older than that.

In addition to herbs, leaves, and flowers, you can make tea out of organic lemons. Below I share some basic techniques for drying these medicinal edibles for teas.

INSTRUCTIONS

- To dry herbs and the like, tie the stems in bundles and hang them upside down. When dried, remove the stems and keep the leaves or buds in airtight containers away from light. Use for your herbal teas.

- To dry lemons, slice the lemons, place them on a baking sheet, and dry them in a convection oven at 125°F (50°C) for 24 hours. A dehydrator also works, but it is difficult to dehydrate fruit in a gas oven. When the fruit is ready, it will be dry and crisp. Dried lemons should be stored in a cool, dry place. They will keep for several months once completely dried.

- To make tea from dried herbs or fruit, put 1 tablespoon in a cup and pour in 1 cup (240 ml) boiling water. Steep for 20 to 30 minutes, then enjoy.

HERBS, FLOWERS, AND LEAVES YOU CAN GROW YOURSELF THAT MAKE GREAT TEAS	
Peppermint	Peppermint is beneficial for stomach problems. It eases cravings as well as an upset or bloated stomach.
Lavender	This calming herb can relieve headaches and depression. Drink lavender tea before bed if you suffer from insomnia.
Dandelion leaves	This is a natural diuretic, so if you feel puffy and easily store excess water weight, make some dandelion tea and drink 1 quart (1 L) every morning for 5 days. The puffiness will magically disappear!
Marigolds	These yellow or orange flowers are easy to grow; the cool thing is that you can eat them! Use the petals to clear up acne and blemishes, or make tea of them to reduce inflammation.
Sage	These thick gray-green leaves prevent flatulence and can improve premenstrual syndrome and moodiness. Inhale this infusion to relieve respiratory problems such as asthma and sore throat.
Thyme	Thyme balances blood pressure level and is relaxing and calming for the whole nervous system. It also has antiviral properties.
Catnip	Catnip is a powerful detoxifier and balances the digestive system. If you suffer from headaches, use catnip for natural pain relief.

HOMEMADE
SUPPLEMENTS

Save money and avoid nasty additives by making your own supplements. The ones in this section are my absolute favorites and much more effective than most of the products you can buy from a store. Everything has been tried and tested many times and is completely safe to use on a daily basis.

ICED LIME DANDELION TEA

Water retention can be the result of PMS, bad sleep, stress, or a sedentary lifestyle. Most people experience mild water retention from time to time, but for some it can be a recurring and troublesome problem. Dandelion tea is a natural and safe diuretic that you can drink whenever you experience excess swelling and bloating. It is very mild, but it will make your kidneys work a bit harder.

■ Yield: 2 quarts (2 L)   ■ Preparation time: 5 minutes, plus 1 hour to steep   ■ Cook time: 5 minutes

INGREDIENTS

2 quarts (2 L) water

3 or 4 dandelion teabags or equivalent amount of loose tea leaves

2 bay leaves

Juice of 1 lime

INSTRUCTIONS

■ Pour the water into a saucepan and add the dandelion tea and bay leaves. Bring to a boil and let it boil for a few minutes, then take it off the heat and let cool and steep for an hour. Remove the bay leaves and teabags, add the lime juice, and place in the refrigerator to chill.

■ Drink when cool.

DETOX *and cleansing*

The most detoxifying diet you can follow is the ketogenic diet. Just by eliminating inflammatory processed and unnatural foods, your body will begin a series of detox processes. Physical exercise is another great tool that revitalizes and detoxifies the body, mostly by sweating and increasing the flow of lymph fluids.

Lymph is the fluid circulating throughout the lymphatic system. It's a vital part of the immune and circulatory systems. Your body is constantly filtering your blood and intestinal fluids to get rid of bacteria, viruses, and toxic waste products. If you have a passive lifestyle, this filtering process slows down and in rare cases might even get stuck. The result is edema, a condition of localized fluid retention that causes tissue swelling.

Detoxing the liver and lymph is a great way to increase energy, shed excess water, and feel better. Liver Cleanse Tea (below) and Lymph Detox Tea (page 280) help speed up the filtration processes of the liver and lymph and accelerate healing.

LIVER CLEANSE TEA

■Yield: 2 quarts (2 L)   ■Preparation time: 5 minutes, plus 1 hour to steep   ■Cook time: 5 minutes

INGREDIENTS

2 quarts (2 L) water

1 teaspoon dandelion powder

1 teaspoon milk thistle powder

1 teaspoon fennel seed

½ teaspoon ground black pepper

5 drops peppermint oil

INSTRUCTIONS

- Place all the ingredients in a saucepan and bring to a boil. Remove from the heat and let the tea cool and steep for an hour.

- Drink the tea hot or cold. I suggest that you drink 2 quarts (2 L) a day for 5 days for full effect; if you like, combine it with other detox procedures. It can be kept at room temperature.

LYMPH DETOX TEA

■ Yield: 2 quarts (2 L)　■ Preparation time: 5 minutes, plus 1 hour to steep　■ Cook time: 5 minutes

INGREDIENTS

2 quarts (2 L) water

5 bay leaves

8 whole cloves

INSTRUCTIONS

- Place all the ingredients in a saucepan and boil for 5 minutes. Remove from the heat and let cool and steep for an hour.

- This detox tea can be ingested for 5 to 7 days; drink 2 quarts (2 L) a day, hot or cold, and store at room temperature.

ELECTROLYTE
sports drink

This caffeine-free sports drink is a lot more efficient at restoring electrolytes than most commercial sports drinks. If you train hard and have been sweating a lot, this drink is perfect for you.

■ Yield: 1 quart (1 L)　■ Preparation time: 3 minutes, plus 1 hour to cool

INGREDIENTS

1 quart (1 L) water

1 teaspoon Himalayan salt

½ teaspoon potassium powder

5 (200-mg) magnesium tablets, powdered, or capsules

Juice of 1 lime

INSTRUCTIONS

■ Bring the water to a boil, then take it off the heat. Add the salt, potassium, and magnesium and allow the minerals to dissolve in the hot water. (If you use capsules, open them and add the contents only.) Add the lime juice, stir, and place in the refrigerator to chill before serving.

VARIATION

■ Substitute green tea, herbal tea, or natural coconut water for the water.

note ────────

I specifically call for Himalayan salt in this restorative recipe because it contains important minerals that are lacking in regular salt. Natural unprocessed salts such as Himalayan salt are very healthy for our bodies and actually lower blood pressure and restore cellular function.

Try this electrolyte drink if you need to hydrate after a day in the sun, if you have a bad hangover, or if you have diarrhea and lose a lot of water.

COCONUT WATER KEFIR DRINK

Water kefir grains are a great source of probiotics; they are created by a colony of yeast and bacteria and have (despite their name) nothing to do with actual grains. You find them in specialized health food stores and at online health and supplement stores. (Note: Do not confuse this type of kefir grain with "milk kefir grains," which require milk to ferment.)

Coconut water kefir is a nice, palatable way of getting your daily dose of probiotics. This recipe contains sugar, and you can leave it out, but you cannot replace it with honey or a sugar substitute. The sugar is added because bacteria love sugar and consume it to create probiotic enzymes. It's a fermentation process that leaves very little, if any, sugar behind when completed.

You can buy coconut water in most grocery stores. It is naturally sweet, so you need only 3 tablespoons of sugar for one whole batch of this drink.

■ Yield: 1 quart (1 L)   ■ Preparation time: 3 minutes, plus 48 hours to ferment and time to chill

INGREDIENTS

1 quart (1 L) coconut water

3 tablespoons granulated cane sugar

¼ cup (60 ml) hydrated water kefir grains

15 drops liquid stevia

note

The sugar will be consumed after 48 hours. If you leave the grains longer, you will starve them. Cooling the drink stops the fermentation process, which means that it needs to be at room temperature while fermenting.

INSTRUCTIONS

■ Heat the coconut water until it is hot, but not yet simmering. Pour it into a 1-quart (1-L) jar, then add the sugar. The sugar will dissolve in the hot coconut water. Add the kefir grains and cover with a clean cloth, affixing the cloth with a rubber band. Leave on the counter at room temperature for 48 hours.

■ Strain the grains through a fine-mesh strainer or coffee filter and pour the drink into a clean, dry container. Add the stevia and put it in the refrigerator to chill before serving. It will keep for up to a week in the fridge.

VARIATION

■ For a more concentrated dose of probiotics and enzymes, just repeat the steps above two or three times. Do not add sweeteners or flavorings until the fermentation process is complete. Don't discard the grains after the drink has finished fermenting; rinse them thoroughly, put them in a jar of water, and put it in the refrigerator. They will keep for weeks.

taste tip

Berries (such as raspberries, blackberries, and blueberries), ginger, and stevia go well with this drink, but absolutely no citrus!

SAUERKRAUT
(PROBIOTICS)

Fermented cabbage, or sauerkraut, is a great fermentation project to do at home. All you need is a jar, cabbage, and salt. The cabbage releases liquid, creating its own brine. Submerged in this liquid, it starts to produce healthy probiotic bacteria and enzymes.

The process takes two to four weeks, so you will need a little patience. During the fermentation process, bacteria convert sugars into lactic acid, and the result is a lot of the same healthy bacteria that can be found in yogurt. The difference is that these bacteria are in much greater vitality and abundance than in most commercial dairy products!

■Yield: 2.2 pounds (1 kg)   ■Preparation time: 15 minutes, plus 2 to 4 weeks to ferment

INGREDIENTS

1½ pounds (700 g) green cabbage, thinly sliced or shredded

3½ ounces (100 g) carrots, thinly sliced or finely diced

1 tablespoon fine sea salt (see notes)

notes

When fermenting foods, the best choice is sea salt. Do not use refined salts or salts with additives, such as iodine or anti-caking agents.

Do not use onions or garlic! They don't go well with fermentation and could ruin your sauerkraut.

INSTRUCTIONS

■ Put the cabbage and carrots in a large bowl. Add the salt and toss to evenly coat, then begin squeezing the cabbage and carrots with your hands. The salt causes them to release liquid, and this liquid will be the fermentation brine. Pack the cabbage and carrot slices into a clean 1-quart (1-L) jar and add the brine; it should cover the vegetables. If it doesn't, add water until the veggies are covered, then add an extra teaspoon of salt. Make sure that it's tightly packed, and use a clean weight to keep the vegetables submerged under the brine. You can use the cabbage core as a weight; it fits perfectly! Make sure to notch a hole in it so that you have a way to pull it up after the fermenting is complete.

■ Cover the jar with a clean cloth and affix with a rubber band. Keep the jar at room temperature; make sure that the temperature doesn't fluctuate more than 10°F (5°C) over the course of the day. The fermentation process will begin in the first 24 hours and continue until you put the jar in the refrigerator. Open the jar after a week and taste the sauerkraut with a clean fork. Fermentation is a safe process as long as you keep the veggies covered with brine and don't contaminate the jar with a dirty fork or fingers.

■ Enjoy your sauerkraut alone or as a condiment. A tablespoon a day is great for your immune system and stomach health!

VARIATION

■ Carrots are a flavoring ingredient. Other flavors that work well with this kind of fermentation process are ginger, radish, caraway seed, dill, parsley, and kale.

CHICKEN BROTH *and collagen*

Homemade broth and collagen supplements contain much more nutrients than the products you can buy, especially if you use bones from quality sources. This broth will get you loads of great-quality collagen, minerals, and amino acids. If you include broth rich in collagen in your weekly meal plan, you can forget about Botox and expensive creams because collagen is an effective and ancient hair and skin treatment that really works!

Always use free-range antibiotic- and hormone-free chicken. You can make collagen out of all kinds of bones, but chicken is my personal favorite, along with oxtail. It's a great use for the leftover carcass from Sunday's roast chicken dinner!

■ Yield: 2 quarts (2 L) ■ Preparation time: 5 minutes, plus at least 2 hours to cool ■ Cook time: 4 to 5 hours

INGREDIENTS

1 chicken carcass

10 chicken feet

2 quarts (2 L) water

1 teaspoon vinegar

tip

If you pour the broth into a silicone mold before it cools, you will get ready-to-eat snack-sized collagen bombs!

INSTRUCTIONS

■ Rinse the chicken carcass and feet, then parboil them for a couple of minutes, and rinse again. Discard the boiling water and rinse the chicken carcass and feet again. Place the chicken carcass and feet in a clean pot and cover with 2 quarts (2 L) of fresh water. Boil for 5 minutes, then reduce the heat to a simmer and add the vinegar. Simmer, covered, for 4 to 5 hours, until it develops a yellowish tone. Add more water if needed to keep the chicken covered.

■ Remove the bones and strain the broth, then transfer it to a container and put it in the refrigerator. When cool, the broth will solidify and look like Jell-O. It will keep for a week in the refrigerator or a month in the freezer.

usage

Eat a tablespoon a day as a nutrient-packed collagen supplement. You can also heat it up and drink it as a soup.

CHEWABLE VITAMINS

Commercial vitamins that look like candy should be avoided at all costs. They generally contain lots of artificial ingredients and very small amounts of actual vitamins.

You can easily make your own chewable vitamins that are healthy and natural and taste great. These are perfect for anyone who has trouble swallowing pills. Suitable vitamins for this are vitamin C, vitamin D, and magnesium. This recipe will yield a safe 200-mg dose per vitamin.

I suggest buying vitamin C powder (ascorbic acid) from a trusted brand. Vitamin D is best absorbed as a liquid, and magnesium could be in pellet, capsule, or powder form.

■ Yield: 100 vitamins ■ Preparation time: 10 minutes, plus 30 minutes to cool
■ Special equipment: Cute silicone molds (I use two 50-cavity bear-shaped molds with a cavity size of 0.8 inch [2 cm] high by 0.4 [1 cm] inch wide by 0.4 inch [1 cm] deep)

INGREDIENTS

Coconut oil, softened, for the mold

8 teaspoons gelatin powder

¾ cup plus 1½ tablespoons (200 ml) sugar-free, non-carbonated juice

0.7 ounce (20 g) vitamin powder of choice

INSTRUCTIONS

■ Grease the inside of each cavity with a small amount of coconut oil so the vitamins won't stick.

■ Mix together the gelatin and juice in a small saucepan. Heat it up, stirring, until the gelatin has completely dissolved. Take the pan off the heat and keep stirring until the mixture thickens a bit. Add the vitamin powder and stir until completely blended.

■ Pour the mixture into the greased molds and place in the freezer to set for 30 minutes. Take them out, pop them out of the molds, and store in a jar in the refrigerator. They will keep for weeks.

tip ——————————

You can use sugar-free lemon, lime, ginger, or blueberry juice or make a small batch in each flavor.

Ketogenic Foods List

PROTEIN	PORTION SIZE	CALORIES (KCAL)	FAT (G)	CARBS (G)	PROTEIN (G)
Bacon	3½ ounces (100 g)	541	42	0	37
Beef	3½ ounces (100 g)	252	15	0	27
Chicken breast	3½ ounces (100 g)	114	2	0	23
Cottage cheese	3½ ounces (100 g)	100	4	2	13
Duck	3½ ounces (100 g)	132	6	0	18
Egg	1 cooked	68	5	0	5
Egg	1 fried	78	6	0	5
Egg white	1 raw	17	0	0	4
Fish fillet (flounder, sole, scrod, etc.)	3½ ounces (100 g)	75	0	0	17
Ham	3½ ounces (100 g)	172	8	0	22
Lamb	3½ ounces (100 g)	292	21	0	24
Pork	3½ ounces (100 g)	240	20	0	16
Salmon	3½ ounces (100 g)	146	6	0	22
Shrimp	3½ ounces (100 g)	144	2	1	28
Tuna	3½ ounces (100 g)	116	1	0	25

OILS AND FATS	PORTION SIZE	CALORIES (KCAL)	FAT (G)	CARBS (G)	PROTEIN (G)
Avocado oil	3½ ounces (100 g)	884	100	0	0
Bacon fat	3½ ounces (100 g)	896	100	0	0
Butter	3½ ounces (100 g)	717	81	0	0
Cream cheese	3½ ounces (100 g)	250	23.5	3	4
Heavy cream (40%)	3½ ounces (100 g)	345	37	3	2
Lard	3½ ounces (100 g)	902	100	0	0
Macadamia oil	3½ ounces (100 g)	718	76	14	8
Mayonnaise, full fat	3½ ounces (100 g)	717	78	3	1
MCT oil	3½ ounces (100 g)	900	100	0	0
Olive oil	3½ ounces (100 g)	884	100	0	0
Olives, black	3½ ounces (100 g)	105	10	6	1
Olives, green	3½ ounces (100 g)	145	15	4	1
Pork rinds	3½ ounces (100 g)	545	31	0	61
Salad dressing, creamy, full fat	3½ ounces (100 g)	528	57	3	1
Sour cream, full fat	3½ ounces (100 g)	193	20	3	2

PORTION SIZE	CALORIES [KCAL]	FAT [G]	CARBS [G]	PROTEIN [G]	VEGETABLES AND FRUITS
3½ ounces (100 g)	20	0	3	2	Asparagus, cooked
3½ ounces (100 g)	107	1	15	7	Beans, cooked (black beans, kidney beans, chickpeas, lentils)
3½ ounces (100 g)	20	0	2	1.5	Beans, green
3½ ounces (100 g)	40	0.5	7	0.5	Blueberries
3½ ounces (100 g)	34	0.4	6	3	Broccoli
3½ ounces (100 g)	41	0.4	7	3.5	Brussels sprouts
3½ ounces (100 g)	50	0.7	6	1	Cabbage, green
3½ ounces (100 g)	41	0.2	9	0.9	Carrots
3½ ounces (100 g)	25	0.1	5	2	Cauliflower
3½ ounces (100 g)	14	0	3	0.7	Celery
3½ ounces (100 g)	15	0.1	3.6	0.7	Cucumber
3½ ounces (100 g)	65	3.9	8	0.8	Eggplant
1 clove	4	0	1	0.2	Garlic
3½ ounces (100 g)	40	0.4	4	3.5	Kale
3½ ounces (100 g)	17	0.2	3.2	1.5	Lettuce
3½ ounces (100 g)	26	0.3	3	3	Mushrooms
3½ ounces (100 g)	32	0.2	7	1.8	Onion, green
3½ ounces (100 g)	40	0	9	0.9	Onion, white
3½ ounces (100 g)	118	0.1	27	3	Potato
3½ ounces (100 g)	52	0.7	11	1.2	Raspberries
3½ ounces (100 g)	72	0.1	17	2.5	Shallots
3½ ounces (100 g)	23	0.4	3.6	2.9	Spinach
3½ ounces (100 g)	68	4.2	7.8	1.7	Squash
3½ ounces (100 g)	32	0.3	7.7	0.7	Strawberries
3½ ounces (100 g)	18	0.2	3.9	0.8	Tomatoes

References

Avena, N. M., R. Pedro, and B. G. Hoebel. "Evidence for sugar addiction: behavioral and neurochemical effects of intermittent, excessive sugar intake." *Neuroscience and Biobehavioral Reviews* 32, no. 1 (2008): 20–39. DOI: 10.1016/j.neubiorev.2007.04.019.

Bijkerk, C. J., et al. "Soluble or insoluble fibre in irritable bowel syndrome in primary care? Randomised placebo controlled trial." *British Medical Journal* 339, no. 7721 (2009): 613–15. DOI: 10.1136/bmj.b3154.

Challem, Jack. *The Inflammation Syndrome: Your Plan for Great Health, Weight Loss, and Pain-Free Living.* Hoboken, NJ: John Wiley & Sons, 2003.

Corti, Maria-Chiara, et al. "Clarifying the direct relation between total cholesterol levels and death from coronary heart disease in older persons." *Annals of Internal Medicine* 126, no. 10 (1997): 753–60.

Devlin, T. M. *Textbook of Biochemistry with Clinical Correlations.* 7th Edition. Hoboken, NJ: John Wiley & Sons, 2010.

Goldbourt, U., S. Yaari, and J. H. Medalie. "Isolated low HDL cholesterol as a risk factor for coronary heart disease mortality: a 21-year follow-up of 8000 men." *Arteriosclerosis, Thrombosis, and Vascular Biology* 17, no. 1 (1997): 107–13.

Graham, N. A., M. Tahmasian, B. Kohli, E. Komisopoulou, M. Zhu, I. Vivanco, et al. "Glucose deprivation activates a metabolic and signaling amplification loop leading to cell death." *Molecular Systems Biology* 8 (2012): 589. DOI: 10.1038/msb.2012.20.

Kannel, W. B., "The Framingham study." *British Medical Journal* 2, no. 6046 (1976): 1255.

Kennedy, G. C. "The role of depot fat in the hypothalamic control of food intake in the rat." Proceedings of the Royal Society of London Series B, *Biological Sciences* 140, no. 901 (1953): 578–92.

Keys, A. "Atherosclerosis: a problem in newer public health." *Atherosclerosis* 1 (1953): 19.

Keys, A. "Seven countries: A multivariate analysis of death and coronary heart disease."

Konstantinov, I. E., N. Mejevoi, and N. M. Anichkov. "Nikolai N. Anichkov and his theory of atherosclerosis." *Texas Heart Institute Journal* 33, no. 4 (2006): 417–23.

Martini, M. C., B. B. Danciasak, C. J. Haggans, W. Thomas, and J. L. Slavin. "Effects of soy intake on sex hormone metabolism in premenopausal women." *Nutrition and Cancer* 34, no. 2 (1999): 133–39.

Norat, T., and E. Riboli. "Dairy products and colorectal cancer: a review of possible mechanisms and epidemiological evidence." *European Journal of Clinical Nutrition* 57, no. 1 (2003): 1–17. DOI: 10.1038/sj.ejcn.1601522.

Oppenheimer, Rebecca. *Diabetic Cookery: Recipes and Menus.* Carlisle, MA: Applewood Books, 2007.

Pencina, M. J., R. B. D'Agostino Sr., M. G. Larson, J. M. Massaro, and R. S. Vassan. "Predicting the thirty-year risk of cardiovascular disease: the Framingham heart study." *Circulation* 119, no. 24 (2009): 3078–84. DOI: 10.1161/CIRCULATIONAHA.108.816694.

Pischon, T., C. J. Girman, F. M. Sacks, N. Rifai, M. J. Stampfer, and E. B. Rimm. "Non–high-density lipoprotein cholesterol and apolipoprotein B in the prediction of coronary heart disease in men." *Circulation* 112, no. 22 (2005): 3375–83. DOI: 10.1161/CIRCULATIONAHA.104.532499.

Siri-Tarino, P. W., Q. Sun, F. B. Hu, and R. M. Krauss. "Saturated fatty acids and risk of coronary heart disease: modulation by replacement nutrients." *Current Atherosclerosis Reports* 12, no. 6 (2010): 384–90. DOI: 10.1007/s11883-010-0131-6.

Stefanidis, Aneta, and M. J. Watt. "Does too much sugar make for lost memories?" *Journal of Physiology* 590, Pt. 16 (2012): 3633–34. DOI: 10.1113/jphysiol.2012.235028.

Stewart, W. K., and L. W. Fleming. "Features of a successful therapeutic fast of 382 days' duration." *Postgraduate Medical Journal* 49, no. 569 (1973): 203–9.

Volek, J. S., M. J. Sharman, D. M. Love, N. G. Avery, A. L. Gómez, T. P. Scheett, and W. J. Kraemer. "Body composition and hormonal responses to a carbohydrate-restricted diet." *Metabolism* 51, no. 7 (2002): 864–70.

Volek, J. S., and S. D. Phinney. *The Art and Science of Low Carbohydrate Performance.* Miami, FL: Beyond Obesity LLC, 2012.

Wu, J. J., J. Liu, E. B. Chen, J. J. Wang, L. Cao, N. Narayan, et al. "Increased mammalian lifespan and a segmental and tissue-specific slowing of aging after genetic reduction of mTOR expression." *Cell Reports* 4, no. 5 (2013): 913–20. DOI: 10.1016/j.celrep.2013.07.030.

Recipe Index

BREAKFAST

128
Keto Swedish Pancakes

129
Quick Crepes

130
Breakfast Porridge

131
Blue Chia Porridge

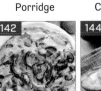
132
Keto Crispbread

134
Classic Oopsies with a Twist

136
Dairy-Free Probiotic Yogurt

138
Granola

140
Bacon and Eggs

141
Scrambled Eggs

142
Savory Mushroom Omelet

144
Avocado Baked Eggs

LUNCH

148
Keto Burgers

150
Shirataki Pesto Noodles

152
Zucchini Boats

154
Spinach Soup with Boiled Eggs

155
Creamy Salmon Soup

156
Egg and Shrimp Salad

158
Shrimp Omelet with Asparagus

160
Moist and Tender Chicken Breast

162
Moist and Tender Chicken Breast with Beet Salad

164
Chicken Lettuce Wrap

166
Chicken Burgers or Meatballs

168
Pan-Fried Salmon Steak with Herb Butter

DINNER

172
Meat-Filled Bell Peppers

174
Creamy Mussels with Sautéed Spinach

176
Colorful Fish Stew

178
Sautéed Chicken Livers with Baby Kale Salad

180
Meat-Filled Keto Tortillas

182
Keto Pizza

184
Steak with Asparagus and Broccoli Mash

SIDES & CONDIMENTS

188
Guacamole

190
Pesto

192
Broccoli Mash

194
Cauliflower Mash

195
Cabbage Mash

196
Eggplant Mash

198
Cauliflower Rice

200
Radish Fries

202
Pumpkin Wedges

203
Coleslaw

204
Marinated Vegetables

206
Ghee

208
Dairy-Free Low-Carb Chips

210
Cheese Chips

212
Hollandaise

214
Béarnaise

216
Mayonnaise

217
Tomato-Olive Spread

218
Tuna Pâté

219
Dried Olives

SNACKS & DESSERTS

222
Chocolaty and Minty Fat Bombs

224
Sour Bombs

226
No-Bake Chocolate Balls

228
Nutty Chocolate Balls

230
Coconut Balls

231
Instant Raspberry Avocado Ice Cream

232
No-Churn Keto Ice Cream

234
Dairy-Free Blueberry Panna Cotta

DRINKS & SMOOTHIES

238
Fatty Coffee

240
Blood Sugar Tea

242
Turmeric Golden Tea

244
Egg Milk

246
Immune Booster Smoothie

248
Ketone Booster Smoothie

250
Sweet Cinnamon Protein Shake

252
Green Protein Shake

254
Creamy Cinnamon Keto Smoothie

256
Blackberry Cheesecake Keto Smoothie

258
Pumpkin Latte

260
Pecan Butter Smoothie

HOW TO...

264
How to Make Whipped Coconut Cream

265
How to Make Coconut Butter

266
How to Make Your Own Flour

268
How to Make Peanut and Nut Butters

270
How to Make Coconut Milk and Nut Milk

272
How to Make Your Own Teas

HOMEMADE SUPPLEMENTS

276
Iced Lime Dandelion Tea

278
Liver Cleanse Tea

280
Lymph Detox Tea

281
Electrolyte Sports Drink

282
Coconut Water Kefir Drink

284
Sauerkraut (Probiotics)

286
Chicken Broth and Collagen

288
Chewable Vitamins

General Index